AF600552

NULLITY IN JUDICIAL ACTS

A Historical Conspectus and a Commentary

THE CATHOLIC UNIVERSITY OF AMERICA
CANON LAW STUDIES
No. 297

Nullity in Judicial Acts

A Historical Conspectus and a Commentary

BY

JOHN J. NOONE, J.C.L.

A DISSERTATION

SUBMITTED TO THE FACULTY OF THE SCHOOL OF CANON LAW OF THE CATHOLIC UNIVERSITY OF AMERICA IN PARTIAL FULFILLMENT OF THE REQUIREMENTS FOR THE DEGREE OF DOCTOR OF CANON LAW

THE CATHOLIC UNIVERSITY OF AMERICA PRESS
WASHINGTON, D. C.
1950

NIHIL OBSTAT:

JOANNES ROGG SCHMIDT, A.B., J.C.D.

Censor Deputatus

Washingtonii, D. C., die 3 novembris 1949

IMPRIMATUR:

✠ D. CARD. DOUGHERTY

Archiepiscopus Philadelphiensis

Philadelphiae die 8 novembris 1949

MURRAY & HEISTER
WASHINGTON, D. C.

PRINTED BY
TIMES AND NEWS PUBLISHING CO.
GETTYSBURG, PA., U. S. A.

TABLE OF CONTENTS

PAGE

FOREWORD ix

CHAPTER

I. HISTORICAL CONSPECTUS 1

Article 1. Roman Law and Early Canonical Legislation 1
Article 2. The Teaching of Gratian 2
Article 3. The Decretal Legislation 5
Article 4. Jurisprudence and Legislation Subsequent to the Decretals and Prior to the New Code of Canon Law 13

CANONICAL COMMENTARY

II. NULLITY BECAUSE OF THE JUDGE'S DEFICIENT JURISDICTION 19

Article 1. Jurisdictional Incapacity 19
Article 2. Deficiencies in Delegated Jurisdiction 21
Article 3. Incompetence of a Judge 25
Article 4. The Exception of Suspicion Raised Against the Judge 33

III. NULLITY BECAUSE OF THE UNLAWFUL CONSTITUTION OF THE TRIBUNAL 36

Article 1. The Judge, the Assessors, and the Auditors 36
Article 2. The Collegiate Tribunal 37
Article 3. The Notary, the Promoter of Justice, the Defender of the Bond, the Couriers, and the Apparitors 39

TABLE OF CONTENTS (Continued)

CHAPTER PAGE

IV. NULLITY BECAUSE OF THE VIOLATION OF CERTAIN PROCEDURAL RULES 42

Article 1. The Circumstances of Time and Place Relative to the Trial 42

A. Terms of Postponement and the *Fatalia Legis* 42

B. The Place of the Trial 43

Article 2. The Recording and the Preservation of the Judicial Acts 46

V. NULLITY BECAUSE OF THE DEFICIENT STATUS OF THE LITIGANTS 49

Article 1. The Right of the Principal Litigants to Stand in Judgment 49

A. Juridic Capacity 49

B. Procedural Capacity 51

1. Minors 52

2. The Insane, Prodigals, and Weak-minded Persons 53

3. Religious 56

4. Moral Persons 58

a.) Non-collegiate Moral Persons .. 59

b.) Secular Collegiate Moral Persons 61

c.) Religious Moral Person 63

C. Legitimation to Act in a Certain Case .. 64

Article 2. Unauthorized Procurators 70

VI. NULLITY IN THE COURSE OF THE TRIAL 80

Article 1. The Bill of Complaint 80

Article 2. The Judicial Summons 81

Article 3. The Joinder of Issue 93

TABLE OF CONTENTS (Continued)

CHAPTER PAGE

Article 4. Nullity in the Development of the Trial — 95
A. Regulations for a Valid Renouncement 95
B. Prejudicial Attempts Against the Rights of the Litigants — 97
C. The Introduction of New Proof After the Closing of the Case — 100

VII. NULLITY IN THE DEFINITIVE SENTENCE — 101
Article 1. Deficiencies in the Definitive Sentence — 101
Article 2. The Interpretation of Canons 1892 and 1894 — 105
A. The Liberal Interpretation — 107
B. The Strict Interpretation — 109
C. The Jurisprudence of the Sacred Roman Rota — 113

CONCLUSIONS — 121

BIBLIOGRAPHY — 123

ABBREVIATIONS — 129

BIOGRAPHICAL NOTE — 130

ALPHABETICAL INDEX — 131

CANON LAW STUDIES — 134

FOREWORD

Nullity in judicial acts is explained as a substantial defect in a trial, or a violation of a procedural regulation which binds under pain of invalidity. Abstractly considered, nullity is a remedy of law, for it is a means of invalidating or having declared void a judicial act about which a competent person complains.

It is not within the scope of this dissertation to treat of the remedy against a sentence that is null and void; the question of the complaint of nullity against a sentence is not taken up here. The dissertation deals rather with the causes of nullity, or the defects in procedure, which invalidate judicial acts and the sentence.

In Roman law the sanction of nullity for a violation of the judicial order was not unknown; however, this dissertation does not propose to give an exhaustive explanation of the causes of nullity in judicial acts according to Roman law. Roman law is considered only in so far as it influenced or was adopted by Canon law in this matter. The early evidence of ecclesiastical legislation on nullity in judicial acts is fragmentary. There are indications that the ancient Church adopted Roman law regulations on procedure. The *Decree of Gratian* contains a rather complete list of the causes of judicial nullity according to Canonical and Roman law sources.

In the legislation of the Decretals there are many canons declaring what elements of a judicial process must be observed in a certain matter under pain of invalidity. After the time of the Decretals there was very little legislation on nullity in judicial acts; hence, for the period from the later Middle Ages down to the time of the Code the dissertation considers rather the doctrinal sources of the law. The doctrine in this matter tended to multiply the causes of nullity in judicial acts to such an extent that the administration of justice was impeded, and that it became difficult for a case to become irrevocably adjudicated, since the complaint of nullity on account of a deficiency in the procedure could be so easily alleged. Gradually, however, the causes of nullity in judicial acts became more restricted in number. In the present legislation their number has been practically reduced to a minimum.

The canonical commentary, Part II, of this dissertation, does not touch the entire procedural law of the Code with a view to investigating where nullity can occur and where it cannot occur in ecclesiastical trials. It relates for the most part to only those procedural norms which are actually invalidating laws. These laws are not many, in view of the present tenor of the Code with reference to the question of nullity. Other laws are treated, but solely because there was some doubt about the nature of the laws, or because an author had suggested that such laws carried with them the sanction of invalidity.

Practicability was also a norm for the selection of the various problems which are treated in this dissertation, for a negative subject, such as judicial nullity is, lends itself to almost un-ending speculation as to its possible obtrusion in a canonical trial. Cases which are not likely to come up in practice are either omitted or given but a summary treatment.

Any consideration of judicial nullity must be ever aware of the regulation of canon 1680: "The nullity of an act is established only when the essential constitutive elements of the act are lacking, or when there are wanting the solemnities or the conditions which are required by the sacred canons under the pain of nullity. The nullity of any act does not comprise the nullity of those acts which precede or follow it and which do not depend upon the act." Hence, in cases of doubt the presumption will always be in favor of validity. It was in accord with the rule of canon 1680 that this dissertation was written.

The writer wishes to express his heartfelt gratitude towards His Eminence, Dennis Cardinal Dougherty, Archbishop of Philadelphia, for the opportunity of pursuing advanced studies; towards the Faculty of the School of Canon Law for their kind direction and valuable assistance; and to all others for their help in making possible the completion of this work.

CHAPTER I

Historical Conspectus

ARTICLE 1. ROMAN LAW AND EARLY CANONICAL LEGISLATION

To insure the administration of justice in judicial procedure, history reveals that it has always been necessary to attach the sanction of nullity to certain regulations governing judicial acts. The transgression of such a regulation furnished cause for the nullity of the judicial process; hence to pronounce a sentence against one who had not been cited or who had not been given an opportunity to defend himself was according to the natural law, to act invalidly, since everyone possessed the natural right to be heard in his own defense. From the earliest times positive law attached the sanction of nullity to certain basic requirements for a just trial. In Roman law the incompetence of the judge,[1] the lack of the *ius standi in iudicio* on the part of the litigants,[2] the omission of the citation or of the joinder of issue,[3] procedure in the absence of the parties except in the case of contumacy,[4] the rendering of a sentence if it was not in writing, the failure of the judge publicly to read the sentence to the parties present,[5] and the obtrusion of a manifest injustice in the sentence were all procedural deficiencies which rendered the trial invalid.[6]

The Church was always careful to declare the invalidity of a

---

[1] *Corpus Iuris Civilis,* Vol. II, *Codex* (10. ed. recognovit et retractavit Paulus Krueger, Berolini: apud Weidmannos, 1929), (7, 48) 1; cf. (7, 48) 2, 4 and (3, 13) 3. (Hereafter referred to as C.)

[2] C. (3, 1) 6.

[3] *Corpus Iuris Civilis,* Vol. III. *Novellae* (5. ed. recognovit Rudolfus Schoell; Opus Schoelii morte interceptum absolvit Guilelmus Kroll, Berolini: apud Weidmannos), 53 (hereafter referred to as N.); cf. C. (7, 45) 4.

[4] D. (42, 47) pr.

[5] C. (7, 44) 1, 2, 3; (7, 45) 6.

[6] C. (7, 64) 1, 2, 5, 7.

procedure when undertaken against an absent person,[7] and, as is evident from the letters of Pope St. Gregory the Great (590-604), a sentence that was manifestly unjust because it was contrary to the law or because of the failure to observe the prescribed judicial order was considered invalid by the ecclesiastical authority.[8]

In 853, Hincmar, the Archbishop of Rheims (845-882), stated that writing was always required, and that an unwritten sentence did not deserve to be called a sentence.[9]

ARTICLE 2. THE TEACHING OF GRATIAN

Much of the procedural legislation in Gratian was supported by pseudo-Isidorian Decretals. This was especially true in regard to the sanction of nullity, inasmuch as one of the purposes of the forgers was to impede the judicial processes of lay people against bishops and clerics.[10] However, except for certain regulations like

---

[7] Council of Chalcedon (451), act. 10—Mansi, *Sacrorum Conciliorum Nova et Amplissima Collectio* (53 vols. in 60, Parisiis, 1901-1927), VII, 206 (hereafter cited as Mansi); cf. Pelagius I, ep. "Chartas quas"—Jaffé, *Regesta Pontificum Romanorum ab condita Ecclesia ad annum post Christum natum 1198* (2. ed. correctam et auctam auspiciis Gulielmi Wattenbach curaverunt S. Loewenfeld, F. Kaltenbrunner, P. Ewald, 2 vols., Lipsiae, 1885-1888), n. 990 (hereafter referred to as Jaffé with the corresponding number of the document); cf. c. 19, C. III, q. 9—*Corpus Iuris Canonici* (editio Lipsiensis secunda, post Aemilii Richteri curas . . . instruxit Aemilius Friedberg, 2 vols., Lipsiae: ex officina Bernhardi Tauchnitz, 1879-1881. Editio anastatice repetita, 1922).

[8] St. Gregorius Magnus, *Registrum Epistularum,* Lib. III, ep. 7—*Monumenta Germaniae Historica, Gregorii I Papae Registrum Epistolarum,* Tomus I, pars II (ed. L. Hartmann, Berolini, 1891), pp. 165-168 (hereafter referred to as *MGH*); Jaffé, n. 1211; cf. *Registrum Epistularum,* Lib. III, ep. 6—*MGH, ibid.,* pp. 163-165; Jaffé, n. 1210; C. 7, C. II, q. 1; *Registrum Epistularum,* Lib. XIII, ep. 47, 50, 49—*MGH, Gregorii I Papae Registrum Epistolarum,* Tomus II, pars II (ed. L. Hartmann, Berolini, 1895), pp. 410-418; Jaffé, n. 1912; c. 1, X, *de procuratoribus,* I, 38; St. Gregorius Magnus, *Registrum Epistularum,* Lib. XIII, ep. 10—*MGH, Gregorii I Papae Registrum Epistolarum,* Tomus II, pars 55, pp. 410-418; Jaffé, n. 1874; c. 13, C. 25, q. 2; Jaffé, n. 1724.

[9] C. 9, C. II, q. 1; Council of Soissons (853), held at the monastery of St. Médard—Mansi, XXV, 983.

[10] Van Hove, *Commentarium Lovaniense in Codicem Iuria Canonici,* Vol. I, Tom. I, *Prolegomena* (2. ed., Mechliniae et Romae: H. Dessain, 1945), p. 306.

that which required seventy-two witnesses before a bishop could be condemned,[11] the doctrine of Gratian was not different from that contained in the letters of St. Gregory the Great.[12]

A condemnation without the observance of the judicial order was invalid.[13] The essential judicial order consisted in the making of the citation, in the granting to the defendant of a period of time within which to consider the complaint, in the joining of issues, in the reception of testimony, and in the judge's decision given in writing.[14] Manifest crimes were excepted from the general rule which specified the judicial order that had to be observed in criminal cases.[15] A manifest crime was one that was known on certain authority and which could readily be proved.[16]

In regard to the question of a judge's incompetence Gratian adopted the Roman Law doctrine[17] that the lack of natural status, the proscription of law, and the usage deriving from social conventions could bar and disqualify certain persons from acting as judges:

> Tria sunt quibus aliqui impediuntur ne iudices fiant: Natura, ut surdus, mutus et perpetuo furiosus, et impubes, quia iudicio carent. Lege, qui senatu motus est. Moribus, feminae et servi, non quia non habent iudicium, sed quia receptum est ut civilibus non fungantur officiis. Verum, si servus, dum putaretur liber, ex delegatione sententiam dixit, quamvis postea in servitutem depulsus sit, sententia ab eo dicta rei iudicatae firmitatem tenet.[18]

Since Gratian pointed to but one exception in his listed series of disqualifications, namely, the case of a slave who was believed to have a free status, it can be deduced that a sentence by any of the others mentioned was held to be null and void. Excommunication likewise disqualified a person from acting as accuser, as witness, or

---

[11] C. 3, C. II, q. 4.
[12] Cf. c. 7, C. II, q. 1.
[13] Rubrica, ante c. 1, C. II, q. 1.
[14] *Glossa Ordinaria* ad c. 1, C. II, q. 1, s. v. *Quidam.*
[15] C. 15, 16, 17, C. II, q. 1.
[16] *Glossa Ordinaria* ad c. 15, C. II, q. 1, s. v. *Manifesta.*
[17] D. (5, 1) 12.
[18] *Dictum Gratiani* ad c. 1, C. III, q. 7.

as judge. "Potest autem dici, Catholicum sententia heretici minime teneri. Non enim potest oris gladio ferire quem accusare vel in quem testificari non valet."[19] The *dictum* of Gratian mentions only heretics, but the canon of Pope Nicholas upon which he was commenting referred to excommunication in general.[20]

The ninth question of the third *Causa* contains certain regulations for criminal trials. These regulations bound under sanction of nullity:[21] The defendant had to be present when the accusation was made against him,[22] had to be given a chance to defend himself,[23] and had to be granted a period of time to consider the charge (*induciae*).[24] The charge had to be made in person by the accuser, and not by letter.[25] The witnesses had to deliver their testimony in person, and they could offer testimony only regarding what had taken place in their presence.[26] The sentence could be issued only when the defendant was present unless his absence was the result of his contumacy,[27] and it had to be drawn up in writing.[28] This same *Causa* mentions, too, that the trial was not to be held outside the province wherein the crime had been committed.[29]

Gratian also set down relative to the trial of bishops such legislation as was supported by pseudo-Isidorian texts. The trial of a bishop was invalid unless it was conducted by twelve judges at a

---

[19] *Dictum Gratiani* post c. 37, C. 24, q. 1.

[20] *Ep. Michaeli Augusto* (865): "Miramur, quomodo excommunicati ad iudicandum recepti sint, cum secundum apostolicos canones sine commendaticiis litteris in sola communione recipi prohibeantur. Absurdum enim est, ut, cui non licet etiam cum minimis iuxta sacras regulas communicare, licet etiam ei de suis pene maioribus iudicare."—c. 37, C. 24, q. 1; Jaffé, n. 2111; Mansi, XV, 194.

[21] Rubrica, ante c. 1, C. III, q. 9.

[22] C. 1, 3, 4, 11, C. III, q. 8. The sources of the individual canons are not put down here, since they are mostly pseudo-Isidorian. Those that are authentic have already been considered in this dissertation in their chronological order.

[23] C. 5, 6, 8, C. III, q. 9.

[24] C. 6, C. III, q. 9.

[25] C. 3, 15, C. III, q. 9.

[26] C. 15, C. III, q. 9.

[27] C. 2, 4, 11, 12, 13, 14, C. III, q. 9.

[28] C. 8, 9, C. III, q. 9.

[29] C. 7, C. III, q. 9.

synod convoked in its due time by the authority of the Pope. When the trial had been concluded, then the case was to be submitted to the Apostolic See for its termination.[30]

Finally, Gratian likewise incorporated in his work mention of the various causes which, as has been previously stated, the Roman law designated as involving the sanction of nullity.[31]

ARTICLE 3. DECRETAL LEGISLATION

In the legislation of the Decretals the grounds for nullity in judicial acts were stated more precisely than in the earlier legislation. There were canons governing the status of the judge: A judge could not function validly when he was publicly under the censure of excommunication.[32] The Decretal law also disqualified for the office of judge slaves, the infamous, and all those with reference to whom some legal impediment existed. Such an impediment resulted from excommunication, from a removal from office, from the fact of being suspect, and from a condition of illiteracy on the part of the candidate.[33]

In regard to judicial competence the Decretals prescribed that a judge needed to have jurisdiction over a case in order to pronounce a valid sentence. Thus a decision if reached by the audience in a court room and accepted as the sentence was declared null and void by Pope Innocent III (1199).[34]

Such a practice had been the customary judicial procedure in the diocese of Poitiers. The practice had arisen in imitation of the Germanic custom in the secular courts for determining the sentence. The people as a whole, or skilled men chosen by the people, had the function of judging while the presiding officer took care of the

---

[30] C. 1, C, 5, q. 4; c. 1, C. 3, q. 8.

[31] Cf. c. 41, § 2, C. II, q. 6; c. 4, § 5, C. III, q. 3.

[32] C. 24, X, *de sententia et re iudicata,* II, 27; A. Potthast, *Regesta Pontificum Romanorum inde ab anno post Christum natum MCXXVIII ad annum MCCCIV* (2 vols., Berolini, 1874-1875), n. 5023 (hereafter referred to as Potthast).

[33] C. 13, X, *de rescriptis,* I, 3; *Glossa Ordinaria* ad h. c., s. v. *impedimento;* Jaffé, n. 17668; c. 13, § 5, X, *de haereticis,* V, 7; IV General Council of the Lateran (1215), c. 3; Mansi XXII, 987.

[34] C. 3, X, *de consuetudine,* I, 4; Potthast, n. 604.

executive functions of the court. The people upon finding out what result in a given case the law demanded, then shaped and formulated the judgment which the judge was to pronounce. The judge was not the author of the judgment, but, once the solution of the case had been reached, he promulgated the judgment as his own command and imparted to it the full force of his magisterial power. Among the Germanic peoples this custom reflected various modifications. When the judgment finders had been appointed by the royal legates along with the co-operation of the community to hold the office for life, they were called *scabini.*[35] Pope Innocent III condemned the institution of the *scabini* which existed in the ecclesiastical tribunal of the Diocese of Poitiers.[36]

This condemnation is pointed out as evidence of the struggle of Canon law against the institutions of the Germanic procedure.[37]

The jurisdiction of a judge was deficient also when the matter in question was beyond the competence of his court. An example of this with reference to the secular judge was the case concerning the right of patronage, if it was so joined to and connected with spiritual issues that it could not validly be defined in a secular court.[38] However, the Church's claim to exclusive competence in cases involving the right of patronage did not go unchallenged. In a constitution of the parliament at Clarendon in 1164, King Henry II of England (1154-1189) asserted against the Church that such litigation belonged to the temporal forum. The matter developed into a great controversy as reflected in the claims made by the Church and the English law.[39]

---

[35] Arthur Engelmann, and Others, *A History of Continental Civil Procedure*, Vol. VII of *The Continental Legal History Series*—published under the Association of American Law Schools (Boston: Little, Brown and Company, 1927), pp. 94, 95, 98.

[36] "Nos igitur attendentes, quod consuetudo, quae canonicis obviat institutis, nullius debeat esse momenti, quum sententia a non suo iudice lata nullam obtineat firmitatem."—c. 3, X, *de consuetudine*, I, 4; Potthast, n. 604.

[37] Engelmann, *op. cit.*, p. 888.

[38] Alexander III (1159-81), *Ep. Henrico Anglorum Regi;* c. 3, X, *de iudiciis*, II, 1; Jaffé, n. 13727.

[39] F. Pollock and F. W. Maitland, *The History of English Law before the time of Edward I* (2 vols., Boston: Little, Brown and Company, 1895), I, 127; W. Blackstone, *Commentaries of the Laws of England*, with notes

Not only the object of the trial but also the status of the litigant and the location of the court were essential factors in determining the competence of the judge.[40]

With regard to the exercise of jurisdiction by a delegated judge it was provided that subsequent to the revocation of his jurisdiction he acted invalidly.[41] He also functioned invalidly when he acted contrary to his mandate or exceeded the powers given him in the rescript,[42] and when he passed sentence on persons not mentioned in the rescript, even if these litigants consented to such a prorogation of his jurisdiction.[43] When the tribunal was a collegiate one its sentence could be invalid for the reason that not all of the appointed judges acted on the case.[44] The legislation regarding the nullity of the action of an incompetent judge or tribunal was summed up in the rule of law: "Ea quae fiunt a iudice, si ad eius non spectant officium, viribus non subsistunt."[45]

The litigants themselves could furnish occasion for nullity in the judicial process. Regularly an excommunicated person had no legal capacity, he had no right to plead a case and could always be repelled by means of an exception raised by the defendant, or also *ex officio* by the judge.[46] Only as a defendant could the excommunicated stand in court.[47] However, the disqualification of excommunicates extended only to those who had contracted a major excommunication, since a minor excommunication debarred a per-

---

and references by Thomas M. Cooley (fourth edition by James DeWith Andrews, 4 vols. in 2, Chicago: Callaghan and Company, 1899), III, 251; IV, 423.

[40] C. 4, X, *de iudiciis,* II, 1; Jaffé, n. 14091; c. 1, *de foro competenti,* II, 2, in VI°; cf. c. 1, X, *de officio legati,* I, 30; Potthast, n. 24064.

[41] C. 29, X, *de officio et potestate iudicis delegati,* I, 29; Potthast, n. 3251.

[42] C. 37, X, *de officio et potestate iudicis delegati,* I, 29; Potthast, n. 7726; cf. c. 22, X, *de rescriptis,* I, 3; and c. 15, *de officio et potestate iudicia delegati,* I, 14, in VI°.

[43] C. 40, X, *de officio et potestate iudicis delegati,* I, 29; Potthast, n. 9555.

[44] C. 16, X, *de officio et potestate iudicis delegati,* I, 29; Jaffé, n. 11867; c. 21, X, *de officio et potestate iudicis delegati,* I, 29; Jaffé, n. 17019.

[45] Bonifatius VIII, Reg. 26, R. J. in VI°.

[46] C. 12, X, *de exceptionibus,* II, 25; Potthast, n. 9613; cf. c. 2, 5, 8, 10, X, *de exceptionibus,* II, 25; and cf. *Glossa Ordinaria* ad c. 1, *de exceptionibus,* 11, 12, in VI°.

[47] C. 7, X, *de iudiciis,* II, 1; Jaffé, n. 14054.

son solely from the reception of the sacraments.[48] If the exception of excommunication was not raised by the defendant during the trial, but was raised only after the case had become irrevocably adjudicated, then no invalidation of the trial followed therefrom. Likewise, if the exception of excommunication was raised during the trial, then the litigation was simply to be deferred; all the previous acts at court retained their valid force, and once the plaintiff was absolved from his censure the case could continue from the stage at which it had been interrupted.[49]

A judicial process could be null as arising on the part of the litigants whenever a procurator acted without a proper mandate. Thus a trial was null and void when the mandate of a procurator had been recalled, and when the latter upon notice of this revocation nevertheless proceeded in the case.[50]

The circumstance of time could give rise to nullity in an otherwise valid process. A trial held on Sundays, or on one of the major feasts,[51] or even on local feasts was invalid even if the parties consented, unless considerations of necessity or of piety demanded that the case be decided on these holy days.[52]

The place where a trial was held could become an occasion for nullity in a judicial process. Gregory X (1271-1276), in the II General Council of Lyons (1274), declared that the judicial processes and especially the sentences of secular judges pronounced in churches were absolutely invalid.[53]

Nullity could arise because of a defect in the judicial process itself. This occurred when an essential form or solemnity as required by law was omitted in the trial.

---

[48] C. 2, X, *de exceptionibus,* II, 25.

[49] C. 1, *de exceptionibus,* 11, 12 in VI°; Mansi, XXIII, 644.

[50] C. 4, X, *de procuratoribus,* 38; Potthast, n. 2995; cf. c. 3, X, *de procuratoribus,* I, 38.

[51] Christmas, St. Stephen, St. John the Evangelist, the Holy Innocents, St. Sylvester, Circumcision, Epiphany, Passion Week, the Resurrection and its octave, the Ascension, Pentecost and the next two days, the Nativity of St. John the Baptist, all the feasts of the Blessed Mother and of the twelve Apostles, St. Laurence, Dedication of Blessed Michael, and All Saints.

[52] C. 5, X, *de feriis,* II, 9; Potthast, n. 9592; cf. *ibidem,* c. 1.

[53] C. 2, *de immunitate ecclesiarum, coemeteriorum et aliorum locorum religiosorum,* III, 23, in VI°; Mansi, XXIV, 99.

The essential parts of a trial were the issuing of the citation,[54] the presentation of the *libellus*,[55] and the joining of issue. The latter was technically defined as the placing of a petition in law and the response to that petition.[56] Without the joining of issue not only the sentence was void, but also the receiving of witnesses as also the taking of their testimony was invalid.[57]

In the decretal law the inverting of the order of the trial furnished grounds for appeal. Thus a judge who took cognizance of a prejudicial exception at the same time that he considered the principal question proceeded contrary to the order of law, which demanded that the exception be considered first. In such a case there was reason for a lawful appeal.[58] The inversion of the judicial order made the sentence voidable. Some of the commentators, however, declared that the failure to observe the proper sequence in the judicial acts during the trial resulted *ipso iure* in invalidity for the judicial procedure.[59]

The judge could not validly pass a sentence against an absent party except in a case of contumacy.[60] Hence, when the absent party proved the cause of his absence to have been legitimate, the sentence had to be retracted.[61]

The manner in which a sentence was delivered could also essentially affect its validity. The sentence had to be issued in writing. The judge himself was obliged to read it to the parties. However, a bishop, on account of the dignity of his person, could have some-

[54] C. 8, X, *de maioritate et obedientia,* I, 33; Potthast, n. 2860.

[55] C. 1, X, *de libelli oblatione,* II, 3; Mansi, XIV, 978.

[56] Potthast, n. 9589; c. un, X, *de litis contestatione,* II, 5; cf. c. 54, X, *de electione,* I, 6.

[57] C. 1, X, *ut lite non contestata non procedatur ad testium receptionem vel ad sententiam diffinitivam,* II, 6; Potthast, n. 370; cf. *ibidem,* c. 2, 4, 5; c. 19, X, *de iudiciis,* II, 1.

[58] C. 19, X, *de iudiciis,* II, 1; Potthast, n. 7512.

[59] Accursius (ca. 1185-1260), *glossa* ad C. (7, 45) 4, s. v. *solitum iudicium ordinem;* Cardinalis Hostiensis (Henricus de Segusio), *Summa Aurea* (Venetiis, 1586), II, *de sententia et re iudicata,* § *Is est ordo.*

[60] C. 10, X, *de sententia et re iudicata,* II, 27; Jaffé, n. 16648; Mansi, XXII, 564.

[61] C. 18, X, *de sententia et re iudicata,* II, 27; Potthast, n. 2446; cf. *Glossa Ordinaria* ad h. c., s. v. *remisissent* et *iustam causam.*

one else read the sentence that he had decreed. Moreover, the judge had to sit when he pronounced the sentence.[62]

The Glossators and Durandus (1237-1296) discussed at length this essential obligation of the judge to sit when he handed down a sentence. They raised such questions as that of a judge seated on a horse when he pronounced the sentence; or of a judge in a high tower with the parties down below on the ground, or also of a judge who physically was not able to take a sitting position. Yet, despite all this discussion it seemed reasonable to accept the opinion of the Glossators, namely, that the obligation could be interpreted in a wide sense, so that the sentence was valid as long as the judge in some way occupied his place in the tribunal: "Satis forte fuit de mente iuris quod sedere intelligatur ut sit in sede sua de plano iudicando quocumque modo ibi moretur."[63]

A sentence that was contrary to the *"ius scriptum"* namely, in opposition to the laws and canons, or one in which error was expressed was *"ipso iure"* invalid. Such a sentence was considered manifestly unjust.[64] Panormitanus pointed out that *leges* meant the civil laws, and *canones* signified the ecclesiastical law, but that civil laws were equal to the sacred canons in the ecclesiastical forum only inasmuch as they had been approved by the Church.[65]

According to Roman law a sentence which was issued expressly contrary to the law was invalid.[66] Roman law made a distinction between the *ius constitutionis* and the *ius litigatoris.* A sentence contrary to the laws of the constitutions was *ipso iure* invalid. Thus, if a judge decided that one could not be excused from an office on

---

[62] Bonifatius VIII (1294-1303); c. 5, *de sententia et re iudicata,* II, 14, in VI°.

[63] *Glossa Ordinaria* ad c. 5, *de sententia et re iudicata,* II, 14, in VI°, s. v. *sedendo;* Durandus, *Speculum Iuris* (3 vols., Venetiis, 1577), lib. II, partic. III, *de sententia,* § 8, n. 10, 11.

[64] C. 1, X, *de sententia et re iudicata,* II, 27; Jaffé, n. 845; Abbas Panormitanus (Nicholaus de Tudeschis, 1386-1453), *Commentaria in Quinque Libros Decretalium* (5 vols. in 7, Venetiis, 1588), lib. II, tit. 27, *de sententia et re iudicata,* c. IX (hereafter this work will be cited as *Commentaria*); Glossa Ordinaria ad c. 9, X, *de sententia et re iudicata,* II, 27, s. v. *manifestam.*

[65] *Commentaria,* lib. II, tit. 27, *de sententia et re iudicata,* c. I, n. 2.

[66] D. (49, 1) 19.

account of his age for the reason that age was not an excusing cause, he pronounced contrary to the *ius constitutionis,* and the sentence was invalid *ab initio*; however, if a judge unjustly pronounced that a man had not proved his age in order to vindicate this excuse, then the sentence was contrary to the *ius litigatoris,* and could only be appealed.[67]

In the question regarding the sentence contrary to law the sources were not consistent. In some instances a sentence with this defect was automatically void, but in others it was only voidable. Thus Alexander III nullified a sentence which was based on a local custom in the diocese of Verona for the reason that this custom was contrary to the canon law. In this particular case the Pope's decree was constitutive rather than declaratory.[68] The same Pope in a letter to the Archbishop of York seemed to make a distinction between a sentence that was *ipso iure* void and one that was voidable. The Pope declared that an iniquitous sentence was to be made void, and that a sentence which was manifestly iniquitous ought not to stand: "Item quum aliqua causa appellatione remota committitur, et sententia fertur iniqua, eam evacuari oportet, nec ei debet stari, si iniquitatem contineat manifestam."[69]

Gonzalez-Tellez (+ after 1673) stated that Hostiensis (+ 1271) and the older writers thought that this canon referred only to sentences which were contrary to the *ius constitutionis,* and therefore automatically invalid; however, he himself thought that the Pope made a distinction between sentences that were voidable and those that were void. A sentence contrary to the equity due to the litigant was unjust and voidable, but a sentence that was manifestly iniquitous was *ipso iure* void.[70]

A sentence was manifestly unjust also if an error was expressed in it. If an error of law was expressed in the sentence it was invalid.

---

[67] D. (49, 8) 1.

[68] *Ep. Theobaldo et Clericis Ecclesiae Sanctae Anastasiae Veronensis:* "Licet usus vel consuetudinis non minime sit auctoritas, nunquam tamen veritati aut legi praeiudicat, praescriptam sententiam . . . revocavimus." c. 8, X, *de sententia et re iudicata,* II, 27; Jaffé, n. 12175.

[69] C. 9, X, *de sententia et re iudicata,* II, 27; Jaffé, n. 13878.

[70] *Commentaria Perpetua in singulos textus quinque librorum Decretalium Gregorii IX* (5 vols., Venetiis, 1756), lib. II, tit. 27, C. 9, n. 1 (hereafter cited *Commentaria*).

For example, if a judge pronounced that an election held by suspended clerics was valid since such clerics were capable of holding an election, his sentence contained a clear error of law, and did not bind.[71] An example which the authors usually gave of a sentence with error expressed in it was one that was taken from Justinian's Code. The submitted example was that of a sentence which declared the will of a person who died before the age of fourteen to be valid before the law.[72]

If the error of the law touched some item extrinsic to the merits of the case, even if it was not expressed, the sentence was *ipso iure* invalid. Panormitanus admitted that there was almost an infinite number of cases wherein this type of error could occur. By way of example he furnished a list of procedural nullities. He considered them as errors of law, and not merely as violations of the rules of procedure. Accordingly, good faith was presupposed in the persons to whom any of the following deficiencies attached: a lack of jurisdiction in the judge, or a lack of personal status of the judge, e.g., because of his excommunication, or some deficiency on the part of the litigants, e.g., on the part of a minor standing in court without the authority of his guardian. For further examples Panormitanus referred to Durandus, whose ten categories of nullity are given below.[73] In the light of this observation that an error of law regarding something extrinsic to the merits of the case made a sentence manifestly unjust and therefore invalid, it can be said that manifest injustice as a cause of nullity included all the other causes of nullity in judicial acts.[74]

---

[71] Cf. c. 8, X, *de consuetudine,* I, 4: Potthast, n. 3590; Reiffenstuel, *Jus Canonicum Universum* (5 vols. in 7, Parisiis, 1864-1870), lib. II, tit. 27, n. 72 (hereafter cited Reiffenstuel).

[72] "Si, cum inter te et aviam defuncti quaestio de successione esset, iudex datus a praeside provinciae pronuntiavit potuisse defunctum et minorem quattuordecim annis testamentum facere ac per hoc aviam potiorem esse, sententiam eius contra tam manifesti iuris forman datam nullas habere vires palam est et ideo in hac specie nec provocationis auxilium necessarium fuit."—C. (7, 64) 2; Durandus, *Speculum Iuris,* lib. II, Partic. III, *de sententia,* § 8, n. 22; Panormitanus, *Commentaria,* lib. II, tit. 27, *de sententia et re iudicata,* c. I, n. 6.

[73] Cf. *infra,* p. 24.

[74] Panormitanus, *Commentaria,* lib. II, tit. 27, *de sententia et re iudicata,* c. 1, n. 4, 5. Cf. *infra,* p. 43.

If the error touched the merits of the case, but was not expressed in the sentence, the sentence was regularly *ipso iure* valid, and unless it was appealed within ten days it became a *res iudicata.* This deduction is based on a canon of Pope Innocent III, who declared that a sentence became law for the litigants if it was not appealed within ten days, as long as it was not expressly contrary to the *ius constitutionis.* In this same canon the Pope stressed the distinction between the law and the rights of the litigants. Just as in Roman law, a sentence contrary to the rights of the litigants was not automatically invalid, but only impeachable.[75]

Perhaps the most significant of all the decretal legislation with regard to nullity in judicial acts was a canon from the council of Vienne (1311-1312). This canon was indirect evidence of the tendency to multiply the causes of judicial nullity. To check this tendency Pope Clement V (1305-1314) instituted the summary process for cases regarding benefices, tithes, matrimony, usury, and other matters related to these. The Pope ordered the shorter form of procedure in such matters in order to restrict the harmful prolongation of disputes which was arising from an overscrupulous observance of the rules pertaining to the judicial order.[76]

ARTICLE 4. THE JURISPRUDENCE AND LEGISLATION SUBSEQUENT TO THE DECRETALS AND PRIOR TO THE NEW CODE OF CANON LAW

The canonists and the writers on Roman law from the thirteenth century onward developed the doctrine regarding nullity in judicial acts. They did so either by stating the essential elements of a trial,[77]

---

[75] C. 13, X, *de sententia et re iudicata,* II, 27; Potthast, n. 292; Glossa *Ordinaria,* ad h. c., s. v. *iudicatum.*

[76] C. 2, *de iudiciis,* II, 1, in Clem. Cf. also H. J. Schroeder, *Disciplinary Decrees of the General Councils* (St. Louis: Herder, 1937), p. 417.

[77] Accursius (1185-1260) listed the essential elements of the judicial order as consisting of the presentation of the *libellus,* of the joining of issue, of the taking of the proper oaths, of the writing and publishing of the testimony of the witnesses, of the writing of the sentence, and of its pronunciation by the judge. If any of these elements was missing, or if they did not take place in the order listed, the sentence was invalid.—*Glossa* ad C. (7, 45) 4, s. v. *solitum iudiciorum ordinem;* cf. also Cardinalis Hostiensis (Henricus de Segusio 1250-1253), *Summa Aurea* (Venetiis, 1568), II, *de sententia*

or by arranging the legislation on nullity, both the canonical and the civil, according to its various causes.[78] As time went on there was a tendency to multiply the causes of nullity. A noteworthy example of this is the oath which the parties took attesting to the fact that they were contesting their respective rights in good faith. The authors mentioned it as essential to a valid trial; yet Boniface VIII explicitly declared that the omission of the oath rendered the judicial process neither void nor voidable.[79]

Vantius, a sixteenth century author, whose work was published in printed form in 1588, arranged the Roman law and canonical legislation on nullities in trials and sentences in fourteen chapters or rubrics. In the first rubric he furnished an explanation of nullity in judicial acts. He described it as a *"defectus rei gestae."* At the same time he stated that in the abstract a nullity could be considered as a right for taking action (*facultas agendi*), as a remedy in law, and as a legal claim, since it implied the possession of a right and the corresponding use of a means to invalidate or to have declared void a judicial act about which a competent person had raised a justified complaint.[80]

The trend in doctrine to multiply the causes of judicial nullity had little effect on the legislative mind of the Church, as is evident from the fact that the Popes reduced the causes of nullity for cases tried in the tribunals of the Papal States to three: The lack of

---

et re iudicata, § *Is est ordo:* Durandus (1272), *Speculum Iuris,* lib. II, partic. III, *de sententia,* § 4, n. 1; Bartolus a Saxoferrato (1359), *Commentaria,* Tomus VIII, *In Secundum atque Tertiam Codicis Partem* (Venetiis, 1590), ad septimum librum Codicis, tit., *de sententiis, et interlocutionibus omnium iudicum,* lex. 4, § 4, 5.

[78] "Nulla autem dicitur sententia multis modis. Ratione iudicis, ratione iurisdictionis, ratione litigatorum, ratione loci, ratione temporis, ratione causae, ratione quantitatis, ratione modi, ratione processus, ratione manifestae iniquitatis."—Durandus, *Speculum Iuris,* lib. II, Partic. III, *de sententia,* § 8; cf. also Ioannes Andreae (before 1338), *In secundum Decretalium Librum Novella Commentaria* (Venetiis, 1581), c. 1, § 7, *de sententia et re iudicata;* Panormitanus, *Commentaria,* lib. II, tit. 27, *de sententia et re iudicata,* c. I, n. 5.

[79] C. 1, *de iuramento calumniae,* II, 4, in VI°.

[80] Sebastianus Vantius, *Tractatus de Nullitatibus Processuum et Sententiarum* (Venetiis: Apud Jacobum Cornettum, 1588), Rub. I, n. 1.

the proper jurisdiction, the omission of the proper citation, and the absence of a sufficient mandate for the procurator of a party to a trial.[81]

De Luca (1614-1683) commended the Apostolic Constitutions for this restriction of the causes of nullity in judicial acts, inasmuch as they eliminated the nullities which had arisen from a too subtle interpretation of the law and from a rigorous insistence on the formalities of procedure.[82]

The restriction of procedural nullities to defects which related to the holding of jurisdiction, to the issuing of the citation, and to the employing of a mandate did not obtain outside the Papal States. Judges elsewhere considered causes other than these three as grounds, *ipso iure,* for the invalidity of judicial acts. Much attention was in fact paid to this problem, so that the doctrine on judicial nullity developed rapidly. One of the principal doctrinal sources is the list of the thirty causes of nullity set down by Robert Maranta (1530) in his work, the *Speculum Aureum.*[83]

The tendency in doctrine to multiply the causes of nullity continued through the seventeenth century. In 1678 the monumental work, *Tractatus de Nullitatibus,* of a Neapolitan lawyer, Blasius Altimarus (1638?-1713), was published. In this specialized treatise all the nullities that could result in judicial procedure were completely catalogued and arranged. The work was divided into fourteen rubrics or titles, which filled two large folio volumes.[84]

---

[81] Const. *In throno iustitiae,* 1561, § 13—*Bullarium Diplomatum et Privilegiorum Sanctorum Romanorum Pontificum Taurinensis Editio* (24 vols., et Appendix, Augustae Taurinorum, 1857-1872), VII, 155 (hereafter referred to as *Bull. Rom.*); Const. *Cum ab ipso,* 1562—*Bull. Rom.,* VII, 214; Const. *Litium dispendiis,* 1593—*Bull. Rom.,* X, 17; Const. *Universi agri,* 1 mart. 1612, § 5, n. 19: "Non attendantur praeterea aliquae nullitates in causis, praeterquam ex defectu iurisdictionis, citationis, vel mandati."—*Bull. Rom.,* XII, 68.

[82] De Luca, *Theatrum Veritatis et Justitiae* (16 vols. in 9, Coloniae Agrippinae, 1706), VII, disc. 38, n. 22-27; cf. also Fagnanus, *Commentaria in Quinque Libros Decretalium* (5 vols. in 3, Venetiis, 1708-1709), lib. II, tit. 27, c. 2, n. 47.

[83] Robertus Maranta, *Speculum Aureum et Lumen Advocatorum Praxis Civilis* (Venetiis, 1590), pars IV, dist. 16.

[84] Blasius Altimarus, *Tractatus de Nullitatibus in XIV Rubricas Divisus* (Neapoli, 1678).

The classical commentators on the Decretal law generally raised the question: When is a trial invalid? In answer to this question they usually listed three categories of nullity: 1) Nullity as arising from a lack of capacity or competence on the part of the judge; 2) nullity as arising from some deficiency in the litigants; and 3) nullity as arising from the failure to observe the required judicial order in the conduct of the trial.[85] The classical commentators also made a distinction between those solemnities which were necessary for the intrinsic validity of the sentence and those which were required for its extrinsic validity.[86] For the intrinsic validity it was necessary that the sentence conform to law, both substantive and procedural law.[87]

For the extrinsic validity of the sentence it was necessary that the parties be cited to receive the sentence, that the sentence be in writing, and that it be pronounced from the written manuscript by the judge seated in the tribunal. The pronouncement of the sentence had to be made in the daytime, but not on a day when judicial procedure had to rest.[88]

The distinction between the intrinsic and the extrinsic validity of the sentence was important in the gradual restriction of the grounds for procedural nullity. By custom the requirements for the extrinsic validity of the sentence could be abolished. Engel (+ 1674) remarked that, though by the general law the omission

---

[85] Schmalzgrueber, *Jus Ecclesiasticum Universum* (5 vols. in 12, Romae, 1843-1845), lib. II, tit. 1, n. 78 (hereafter cited Schmalzgrueber), cf. Schmier, *Ius Canonicum Universum* (Venetiis, 1754), lib. II, tract. I, n. 57-59 (hereafter cited Schmier); V. Pichler, *Jus Canonicum* (Ravennae, 1741), lib. II, tit. 1, n. 17 (hereafter cited Pichler); cf. also Gonzalez-Tellez, *Commentaria,* lib. II, tit. 27, c. 1, n. 7, and c. 9, n. 1; Carolus Pellegrini, *Praxis Vicariorum et Omnium in Utroque Foro Iusdicentium* (Venetiis, 1706), pars II, sec. II, subsect. I, n. 79; Reiffenstuel, lib. II, tit. 27, n. 27.

[86] Pichler, lib. II, tit. 27, n. 9, 10; Schmier, lib. II, tract. III, c. 12, n. 43.

[87] Enricus Pirhing, *Jus Canonicum in V Libros Decretalium* (ed. novissima, 4 vols., Dilingae, 1722), lib. II, tit. 27, nn. 4-26 (hereafter cited Pirhing; Schmalzgrueber, lib. II, tit. 27, n. 41, 42.

[88] Reiffenstuel, lib. II, tit. 27, n. 57-104; Schmalzgrueber, lib. II, tit. 27, n. 26-61; L. Engel, *Collegium Universi Juria Canonici* (ed. nova, Beneventi, 1760), lib. II, tit. 27, nn. 6-10 (hereafter cited Engel); Pichler, lib. II, tit. 27, n. 9, 10; Schmier, lib. II, tract. III, c. 12, n. 43-82.

of these solemnities gave rise *ipso iure* to nullity, in his time it was becoming ever more and more necessary to consider the reasonable customs and the *stylus curiae* of the individual tribunals.[89]

Pichler (1670-1736) more explicitly pointed out that custom could prevail against the judicial solemnities required for the extrinsic validity of the sentence, as in many places it actually did. The usage of the individual tribunals in this regard was to be observed. He added that in the imperial court no procedural nullities were adverted to as long as the merits of the case were sufficiently evident. He likewise intimated that according to report the same practice was followed in the Roman Curia, inasmuch as the supreme authority of the Pope sufficed to supply for any omitted judicial solemnities.[90]

In the pre-Code period and subsequent to the decretal legislation the only new general law which bore the sanction of nullity was the law requiring the presence of the defender of the bond in matrimonial cases.[91]

The more recent of the pre-Code authors who considered to some extent the question of nullity in judicial acts were Bouix (1808-1870),[92] Wernz (1842-1914),[93] and Cardinal Lega (1860-1935). This latter author stressed the importance of determining the validity of judicial acts, but warned that the omission or imperfect placing of some act did not necessarily invalidate the entire process.[94] Thus did he anticipate the legislation of the New Code

[89] Engel, lib. II, tit. 27, n. 6; cf. Reiffenstuel, lib. II, tit. 27, n. 69; Schmier, lib. II, tract. III, c. 12, n. 76.

[90] Pichler, lib. II, tit. 27, n. 10; cf. Pirhing's statement: "Nisi per consuetudinum contrarium sit introductum, per quam tolli possunt ejusmodi solemnitates."—lib. II, tit. 27, n. 23.

[91] Benedictus XIV, const. *Dei miseratione,* 3. nov. 1741—*Corpus Iuris Canonici Fontes cura Emi Petri Card. Gasparri editi* (9 vols., Romae [postea Civitate Vaticana]: Typis Polyglottis Vaticanis, 1923-1939 (Vols. VII-IX ed. cura et studio Emi Iustiniani Card. Seredi), n. 381 (this collection will hereafter be cited as *Fontes*).

[92] D. Bouix, *Tractatus de Judiciis Ecclesiasticis* (2. ed., 2 vols., Parisiis, 1866), II, 405-407.

[93] F. X. Wernz, *Ius Decretalium* (2. ed., 6 vols. in 10, Romae et Prati, 1906-1913), Tom. V, lib. I, n. 709.

[94] Michael Lega, *De Iudiciis Ecclesiasticis* (4 vols., Romae, 1896-1901), vol. I, lib. I, nn. 250, 251.

of Canon Law, which states in canon 1680: "The nullity of an act is established only when the essential constitutive elements of the act are lacking, or when there are wanting the solemnities or the conditions which are required by the sacred canons under the pain of nullity. The nullity of any act does not comprise the nullity of those acts which precede or follow it and which do not depend upon the act."

CANONICAL COMMENTARY

CHAPTER II

NULLITY BECAUSE OF THE JUDGE'S DEFICIENT JURISDICTION

ARTICLE 1. JURISDICTIONAL INCAPACITY

Judicial jurisdiction is the power to hear and determine a suit. It consists in the function of judging in trials, namely, to examine and define a controverted issue. Its source is rooted in the determining of the issues of a matter in dispute; its object is to solve a controversy and to terminate a trial by means of a definitive sentence.[1] The test of jurisdiction is whether the judge or the tribunal has the legal right to hear and decide a controversy.

If a judge or a tribunal lacks this right, then any attempted judicial procedure is invalid. The first consideration in this regard is that of jurisdictional incapacity. This incapacity can arise from the natural law or from positive law. By the natural law those who are destitute of the use of reason are incapable of possessing ecclesiastical jurisdiction. Likewise those who, because of illness or old age, lack sufficient powers of discretion are unable to possess or to exercise ecclesiastical jurisdiction.[2]

Infidels and women are absolutely excluded from possessing ecclesiastical jurisdiction. More probably they are excluded by the Divine law, and certainly they are disqualified by canonical practice and legislation.[3] Canon law prescribes also that only clerics can obtain ecclesiastical jurisdiction. Consequently lay persons are disqualified from enjoying this right.[4] Clerics who have been reduced

---

[1] Roberti, *De Processibus* (2 vols., Vol. I, 2. ed., Romae: Apud Custodiam Librariam Pontificii Instituti Utriusque Iuris, 1941; Vol. II, 1. ed., Romae: Apud Aedes Facultatis Iuridicae ad S. Apollinaris, 1926), I, n. 46; cf. canons 1552, §§ 1, 2; 1728; 1729, §§ 1, 2; 1873.

[2] Reiffenstuel, lib. I, tit. 29, nn. 66-73.

[3] Roberti, *De Processibus,* I, n. 94.

[4] Canon 118.

to the lay state are under this same disqualification, since they have lost their clerical rights.[5]

Also debarred from the exercise of ecclesiastical jurisdiction are persons who are laboring under certain canonical penalties. Those who are excommunicated upon the intervention of a condemnatory or a declaratory sentence cannot validly obtain or exercise jurisdiction.[6] A *Vitandus,* moreover, loses entirely whatever power he had previously possessed.[7] Those who by sentence are suspended cannot validly obtain jurisdiction;[8] If persons are suspended by sentence from the exercise of jurisdiction, any act of jurisdiction which they place is invalid. If they are suspended by sentence from an office to which jurisdiction is attached, likewise any act of jurisdiction undertaken by them is invalid.[9] Those who by sentence are personally interdicted cannot validly obtain jurisdiction.[10] Those who are branded with legal infamy (*infamia iuris*) are disqualified from obtaining or exercising jurisdiction.[11] Clerics who are under the peculiar penalty of disqualification for clerical offices and functions cannot obtain jurisdiction.[12] The penalties of deposition and degradation carry with them the absolute disqualification for enjoying any kind of judicial power.[13]

It should be noted, however, that the deficiencies which arise through disqualifications that have been imposed by the ecclesiastical law leave room for the possession of the needed jurisdiction, for this is supplied by the Church in cases of common error and also in cases of positive and probable doubt, whether in relation to the law itself or to some fact comprehended under the law.[14] Unless jurisdiction is supplied, the judicial acts of one who in law is incapable of jurisdiction are invalid, and only the Roman Pontiff, in virtue of his supreme authority, can convalidate a process that

[5] Canon 213, § 1.

[6] Canons 2265; 2264.

[7] Canon 2266.

[8] Canon 2283.

[9] Canon 2279, §§ 1, 2, 1°; 2284.

[10] Canon 2275, 3°.

[11] Canon 2294, § 1.

[12] Canon 2298, § 5.

[13] Canons 2303; 2305.

[14] Canon 209.

is null because of a lack of the requisite jurisdiction. He can effect this convalidation, because he has the power to dispense from all ecclesiastical laws. A bishop cannot, because ordinarily he is unable to relax the general laws of the Church.[15]

ARTICLE 2. DEFICIENICES IN DELEGATED JURISDICTION

One of the synodal or pro-synodal judges may be employed as a delegated judge, or a worthy and qualified priest may be delegated to perform certain judicial acts.[16] For instance, a delegated judge can receive the depositions of witnesses who reside at a considerable distance from the seat of the tribunal and for that reason cannot journey there without extraordinary expense.[17] A delegated judge can effect the joining of issue; he can administer the oaths to the litigants; he can examine witnesses; he can carry out the judicial access and inspection.[18] Hence the delegated judge can perform many of the acts of the trial, so that not the entire collegiate tribunal needs to be present for all the acts of the case. Of course, the acts of a delegated judge are invalid unless they are drawn up by a notary, or at least are subscribed by him.[19]

Judicial nullity may arise because of a deficiency in the delegated jurisdiction of a judge. This deficiency may be in the delegating authority, or in the delegate; or it may arise because the delegate exceeds the terms of his mandate, or because of the expiration of his mandate. With reference to the delegating authority nullity arises if he is not able to delegate jurisdiction. Only persons who possess ordinary judicial power, e.g., the Holy See or the local ordinary, can delegate jurisdiction to a priest over all cases in which his tribunal is competent, or over all cases of a certain kind, or for individual trials.[20] The vicar general cannot delegate judicial jurisdiction, since ordinarily he himself does not possess it.[21] It is seriously doubted whether the *officialis* can delegate his power

[15] Cf. canon 1683; Roberti, *De Processibus,* I, n. 254.
[16] Cf. canon 1581; Roberti, *De Processibus,* I, n. 110.
[17] Canon 1773, § 1.
[18] Canons 1727, 1622, § 3; 1773, § 1; 1807.
[19] Canon 1585.
[20] Canons 199, § 1; 1607.
[21] Canon 1573, § 1.

either entirely or partially. Roberti argues that he cannot delegate his office, since it was given to him in view of his personal qualifications.[22] However, when *vice-officiales* have been duly appointed, they also are part of one and the same tribunal with the bishop and share in his ordinary power. Consequently there is no reason why they cannot sometimes or for some cases take the place of the *officialis* in the diocesan tribunal.[23]

Tobin points out that[24] some general legislation is desired which would expressly state whether the *officialis* can delegate his power partially, i.e., in the sense that the delegated judge would decide the case and pronounce the sentence, for the *officialis,* as any judge, can appoint an auditor, i.e., someone to prepare the various judicial acts for the case which he tries, if the ordinary has not already provided one.[25] Tobin offers several indirect and negative arguments which indicate that the *officialis* cannot delegate his power. The most cogent of his reasons is the one based on canon 1607, viz., that the Code acknowledge as delegated judges only those who are commissioned by the Holy See or by the local ordinary. Hence, the safer opinion is that the *officialis* cannot delegate his power even in part.[26]

Unless a delegated judge has been appointed with a general faculty to try all cases, or all cases of a certain kind, he cannot validly subdelegate another to judge an individual case unless this faculty has been expressly granted to him.[27] Hence, the synodal or pro-synodal judges of the diocese tribunal, since they are delegated judges, and in as much as the law does not provide that they should be appointed with a general faculty to try all cases or all cases of a certain kind, cannot subdelegate their jurisdiction. A synodal

---

[22] Roberti, *De Processibus,* I, n. 99; cf. canon 199, § 2.

[23] Canon 1573, § 3; Lega-Bartoccetti, *Commentarius in Iudicia Ecclesiastica iuxta Codicem Iuris Canonici* (3 vols., Romae: Anonima Libraria Cattolica Italiana, 1938-1941), I, 38 (hereafter cited *Commentarius*).

[24] *De Officiali Curiae Dioecesanae* (Romae: Apud Aedes Pontificiae Universitatis Gregorianae, 1936), pp. 175, 176.

[25] Canons 1580, § 2; 1582.

[26] Tobin, *loc. cit.*

[27] Canon 199, §§ 3, 4.

judge can, however, appoint an auditor for a case that he is hearing if one has not been provided by the ordinary.[28]

A judge delegated by the Holy See, i.e., by the Roman Pontiff, or by the Roman Rota or Apostolic Signatura, cannot subdelegate another as judge if the tenor of the document of delegation declares that he was delegated in view of his special aptitude to act as judge in this case or if the rescript forbids subdelegation of the jurisdiction that it has granted to him.[29]

With reference to the delegate, nullity arises if he is incapable of possessing or exercising ecclesiastical jurisdiction. For instance, one who is excommunicated upon the intervention of a declaratory or a condemnatory sentence cannot validly be delegated as judge.[30] Nullity also arises in connection with a delegated judiciary when several persons have received delegated jurisdiction to proceed in the fashion of a collegiate tribunal, and as a matter of fact one or the other of them is absent from the trial so that not all of them act on the case. However, the terms of the mandate of delegation can provide otherwise than is stated here.[31] Nullity arises, too, on the part of a prospective delegate of the Holy See when he performs the acts of the prospective jurisdiction before he has been officially notified that the jurisdiction has been granted.[32]

With reference to the mandate of delegation, nullity arises when the delegate exceeds the terms of the mandate. If he acts beyond the powers of his commission, either with reference to its jurisdictional content or in relation to the persons over which he has received jurisdiction, he acts invalidly. A mere deviation from the method of transacting the affair, as desired by the delegating authority, is not considered a transgression of the limits of the powers of the mandate except when the method was prescribed as a condition of the delegation.[33] Thus if a pastor has been delegated to examine witnesses in a marriage case, and he also instituted an examination of the parties, this latter act is invalid; however, if he

---

[28] Canons 1574, § 1; 199, § 3; 1580, § 1.

[29] Canons 199, § 2; 1606.

[30] Canons 2264, 2265; cf. *supra*, p. 64.

[31] Canon 205, § 3.

[32] Canon 53.

[33] Canon 203.

examined the witnesses separately or together, he would not necessarily be acting invalidly.

Nullity arises with reference to the expiration of the delegate's mandate whenever the mandate has actually expired and he nevertheless places some judicial act. It is necessary then to investigate the ways in which his mandate may expire; canon 207, § 1. His mandate expires first of all when its terms have been fulfilled. For instance, a mandate to conduct a certain case expires when the trial is terminated by the definitive sentence,[34] or when the case comes to an end by abatement,[35] or through a renouncement or repudiation of the suit.[36] His mandate also expires when the very purpose for its possession and exercise has ceased to exist. This would be the case if the suit came to an end by means of a compromise or through arbitration.[37]

When delegation is granted for a definite period of time and this period lapses, the power of the delegated judge ceases.[38] A delegated judge loses his power also when the delegating authority recalls his jurisdiction; however, the delegate must be directly informed that his power has been recalled before the revocation can take its effect. A delegate may resign his jurisdiction. Before it is effective such a resignation must be directly conveyed to the delegating superior and accepted by him. If delegation is granted *ad beneplacitum* and the delegating authority retires from office, the jurisdiction of the delegate ceases if he has not yet begun to use it. Such would be the case if he had not done so much as to issue the summons.[39]

Judicial acts which a delegated judge performs after the expiration of his power are patently invalid, for only if the power had

---

[34] Canon 1873, § 1, 1°.

[35] Canon 1736.

[36] Canon 1740.

[37] Cf. canons 1925-1932.

[38] Canon 207, § 1.

[39] Canons 207, § 1; 61; 1725, 1°; cf. Coronata, *Institutiones Iuris Canonici* (5 vols., Taurini-Romae: Marietti, 1936-1946. Vols. I and II, 2. ed., 1939; Vol. III, 2. ed., 1941; Vol. IV, 2. ed., 1946; Vol. V, 1936), I, n. 290, p. 352 (hereafter cited *Institutiones*). Hanssen, *De Sanctione Nullitatis in Processu Canonico* (Romae: Apollinaris, 1939), p. 48.

been granted for the internal forum is it still validly exercised when through inadvertence a priest has not noticed that the time for which he was given faculties has elapsed, or that the number of cases for which he was delegated has been exhausted.[40]

Delegated jurisdiction which is granted directly to a person ceases with the death of that person, and it expires with his going out of office if he possessed it in view of his office, notwithstanding the fact that it was given to him personally. Functional jurisdiction, i.e., that which is attached to an office, does not cease with the death of the delegate or with his loss of office, but it passes on to his successors.[41]

When the jurisdiction of a delegated judge has expired in any of the foregoing ways and he attempts to exercise some judicial act, then his acts have no value in the external ecclesiastical forum, unless for some reason the Church has supplied for his lack of jurisdiction. Since he is devoid of any public power for judicial affairs, he is absolutely incompetent to exercise judicial jurisdiction. Consequently any and all such attempted judicial acts remain irremediably null.[42]

ARTICLE 3. INCOMPETENCE OF A JUDGE

All judges who have been legitimately appointed have jurisdiction or the power to render a judicial sentence. Outside the Roman Pontiff, however, no other judge has the power of adjudicating all the cases that pertain to the ecclesiastical forum, nor does any such judge enjoy the right to exercise his power over all the persons subject to ecclesiastical jurisdiction. In order to safeguard the judiciary order for the common good and also for the convenience of the litigants, each judge or tribunal is assigned a portion of the universal jurisdiction of the Church.[43] This portion of the universal jurisdiction determines the competence of the individual judge.[44]

Competence according to canonical jurisprudence is that definite jurisdiction by which a certain tribunal is empowered to judge a

[40] Canon 207, § 2.

[41] Cf. canon 66, § 2; Coronata, *Institutiones,* I, n. 290, p. 532.

[42] Cf. canons 207; 209; 1892, 1°.

[43] Cf. Wernz-Vidal, *Ius Canonicum,* VI, n. 46.

[44] Roberti, *De Processibus,* I, n. 60.

specific case of certain individuals in a determined territory. Not all tribunals can settle all trials indiscriminately. The nature of the case, the persons involved, the remedy sought, and the territorial extent of the jurisdiction are essential factors in the determination of a judge's competence. Hence a diocesan tribunal can render a judicial sentence in only those cases which are subject to its jurisdiction according to the rulings of Canon law.[45]

Incompetence then is a deficiency in the jurisdiction which disqualifies a judge for deciding a case either in view of the nature of that case, or of the status of the litigants, or of the legal action that is petitioned, or of the locale in which the judge holds court. Judicial incompetence is either absolute or relative. It is absolute if the judge is entirely devoid of jurisdiction over a particular case; on the other hand, he may possess jurisdiction, but as a matter of fact he enjoys no title recognized in law for exercising his jurisdiction to decide the particular case which is submitted to him. In such a case his incompetence is relative.[46]

Since a sentence which is issued by an absolutely incompetent judge is irremediably null, it will be necessary to examine the causes of absolute incompetence.[47]

A judge may be absolutely incompetent in certain cases because of the dignity of the persons involved. Thus no human authority can judge the Supreme Pontiff.[48] In order that anyone be brought to trial it is required that he be subject to the jurisdiction of the judge, but by the divine constitution of the Church the Supreme Pontiff is not subject to any human authority either of a physical or of a moral person.[49] Only the Roman Pontiff enjoys this im-

---

[45] Cf. William Doheny, *Canonical Procedure in Matrimonial Cases* (2 vols., Vol. I, *Formal Judicial Procedure*, 2. ed., Milwaukee: The Bruce Publishing Company, 1948), I, 15 (hereafter cited *Canonical Procedure*, I); Burke, *Competence in Ecclesiastical Tribunals*, The Catholic University of America Canon Law Studies, n. 14 (Washington, D. C.: The Catholic University of America, 1922), p. 13.

[46] Wernz-Vidal, *Ius Canonicum*, VI, n. 47; cf. Roberti, *De Processibus*, I, n. 60; Lega-Bartoccetti, *Commentarius*, I, 38.

[47] Canon 1892, 1°.

[48] Canons 1556; 1558.

[49] Alphridus Ottaviani, *Institutiones Iuris Publici Ecclesiastici* (2 vols., Vol. I, *Ius Publicum Internum*, 3. ed., Romae: Typis Polyglottis Vaticanis, 1948), I, n. 217, p. 409; Lega-Bartoccetti, *Commentarius*, I, 31.

munity from judgment. Persons who aid him in the government of the Church, i.e., the personnel of the Roman Congregations, Tribunals, and Offices, are not included in the term *Prima Sedes* in canon 1556, for such persons can be and have been on trial in church courts.[50]

The dignity which certain secular rulers enjoy in virtue of their high offices makes inferior ecclesiastical judges absolutely incompetent in the judicial affairs of these rulers which pertain to the ecclesiastical forum. All judges except the Roman Pontiff are absolutely incompetent to decide the cases of those persons who hold the highest government rank in the nation. They are also incompetent to judge the cases of the wives, of the sons, and of the daughters of these rulers. They have no competence either over the cases of those who have the immediate right of succession.[51]

In the United States, then, all contentious or criminal cases which in the ecclesiastical forum touch the president, the vice-president, the governors or the lieutenant-governors of the states, their wives, or their children, are withdrawn from the jurisdiction of judges inferior to the Roman Pontiff.[52]

Judges inferior to the Roman Pontiff are also absolutely incompetent to judge the cases of cardinals from the day of their promotion in consistory to the cardinalitial rank.[53] They likewise cannot hear and decide the cases of legates of the Apostolic See as long as these legates remain in office. Hence they are incompetent with regard to the cases of legates *a latere,* of nuncios, of internuncios, and of apostolic delegates. However, the cases of those who have merely the honorific title of apostolic legate are not reserved to the Supreme Pontiff.[54] Finally, they cannot judge the criminal cases of bishops, not even those of titular bishops.[55]

Although all judges of intermediate rank are absolutely incompetent to adjudicate the reserved cases listed in canon 1557, § 1, the

---

[50] S.R.R., *Causa Stipendii,* 13 ian. 1913—*AAS,* V (1913), 97; Wernz-Vidal, *Ius Canonicum,* VI, n. 49; Roberti, *De Processibus,* I, n. 63.

[51] Canons 1557, § 1, 1°; 1112; 1558.

[52] Doheny, *Canonical Procedure,* I, 512, 513.

[53] Canons 1557, § 1, 2°; 239, § 1; 1558.

[54] Canons 1557, § 1, 3°; 266; 267; 270; 1558.

[55] Canon 1557, § 1, 3.

Roman Pontiff does not need personally to take cognizance of such cases. He is accustomed to delegate them to one of the Sacred Congregations or to a commission of cardinals.[56]

Incompetence because of the dignity of the persons involved arises also when judges and tribunals inferior to the tribunals of the Holy See decide the cases of persons mentioned in canon 1557, § 2. This canon states that the contentious cases of residential bishops are reserved to the tribunals of the Holy See. Contentious cases, though, which involve the temporal rights or goods of the bishop, or of the episcopal *mensa,* or of the diocesan curia, can be referred to the diocesan collegiate tribunal or carried to the immediately higher court.[57] Cases in which the bishop, as ordinary or extraordinary administrator, represents a moral person which is subject to his jurisdiction are not reserved to the tribunals of the Holy See.[58]

Since contentious cases regarding the temporal rights or goods of a residential bishop are not reserved, the question turns about what contentious cases with reference to him are reserved. The expression "temporal rights and goods" has a rather wide scope; however, as Lega-Bartoccetti indicate, it does not include cases regarding the personal status of the bishop. Hence, such judicial questions as whether or not the bishop is legitimate by birth, or whether he is the rightful heir of a particular person, are reserved to the tribunals of the Holy See.[59]

Judges of courts which are inferior to the tribunals of the Holy See are also absolutely incompetent for judging the cases of dioceses and other ecclesiastical moral persons which do not have a superior below the Roman Pontiff.[60] Hence, the cases of exempt religious communities, whether their members profess solemn vows or simple vows, as long as such communities are withdrawn from the jurisdiction of the local ordinary, come under this reservation. The cases of monastic congregations are also reserved to the tri-

---

[56] Cf. canon 1962; Roberti, *De Processibus,* I, n. 63.

[57] Canon 1572, § 2.

[58] Canon 1653, § 5; Roberti, *De Processibus,* I, n. 63, p. 185.

[59] *Commentarius,* I, p. 36, n. 2.

[60] Canon 1557, § 2, 2°; 1558; Wernz-Vidal, *Ius Canonicum,* VI, n. 49.

bunals of the Holy See.[61] The cases are reserved only when the diocese or the exempt religious community in its entirety is a party litigant, for canon 1579 authorizes the ordinary lower tribunals for the settlement of cases which involve the various subdivisions of religious communities, and canon 1572, § 2, allows a diocesan collegiate tribunal to decide cases involving the temporal rights or goods of the diocese.

Other moral persons which do not have a superior below the Roman Pontiff are the Sacred Congregations and Offices of the Roman Curia; the colleges of the protonotaries apostolic, of the auditors of the Sacred Roman Rota, of the clerics of the Reverend Apostolic Camera, and of the voting prelates of the Apostolic Signatura; and other institutes in Rome and elsewhere whose immediate superior is the Supreme Pontiff.[62]

Roberti states that the reservations of cases to the Holy See as deriving in consequence of the dignity of a person obtains only when that person is the defendant in the trial, inasmuch as the plaintiff must follow the forum of the defendant.[63] This interpretation seems hardly tenable, for at least in part it would defeat the purpose of the reservation. If a case were not reserved when a high-ranking personage acts in the capacity of plaintiff, such a plaintiff could unduly use his position for influencing the judiciary of the lower tribunal to the detriment of the defendant. Moreover, the canon which states: "Actor sequitur forum rei," by its very position in the Code obviously relates to what follows it, viz., the question of relative competence, and accordingly it should not be considered applicable to the preceding canons, which deal with the reservation of cases to the Holy See.[64]

---

[61] Canon 1557, § 2, 2°; Roberti, *De Processibus,* I, n. 64, p. 186.

[62] Roberti, *De Processibus,* I, n. 63, p. 186. Roberti (*loc. cit.*) also lists certain physical persons who in virtue of their office are immediately subject to the tribunals of the Holy See. Such are the secretaries and assessors of the Sacred Congregations, the apostolic protonotaries *de numero participantium,* the auditors of the Sacred Roman Rota, the clerics of the Reverend Apostolic Camera, and the voting prelates of the Apostolic Signatura if they have a domicile in Rome.

[63] Roberti, *De Processibus,* I, n. 63, p. 187.

[64] Canon 1559, § 3.

Other cases become reserved to the Roman Pontiff by the very fact that he summons these cases to his own tribunal. He can do this in virtue of his immediate jurisdiction over all the faithful. He can summon their cases to himself whether they be contentious or criminal, and at any stage of the trial, and he can commit them to whatever judges he may choose. Such action on the part of the Supreme Pontiff renders the lower tribunal absolutely incompetent.[65]

A judge may be absolutely incompetent to decide a controversy because of the nature of the matter of the case. Some cases are reserved in view of the matter that is involved; thus cases which are brought to the Holy See concerning the Pauline privilege are absolutely reserved to the Sacred Congregation of the Holy Office.[66]

A judge may be absolutely incompetent with reference to the judicial functions that he is called upon to perform.[67] Functional incompetence has to do with the instance of the trial, the remedies of law against the sentence, and the execution of the sentence. The discussion which follows will concern those judicial functions which are reserved to a specific tribunal. They are not necessarily reserved to the judge of that tribunal personally. Rather, they are reserved to his tribunal. For some functions more than one judge is competent, but his actual use of that competence rules out the competence of all the others. The writer will seek to show that the other judges are to such an extent absolutely incompetent for the performance of these functions that their attempted performance of them would leave their actions plainly invalid.

Incompetence exists in regard to the instance of the trial when a judge who has taken cognizance of a case in one instance attempts to adjudicate the same case in another instance.[68] Incompetence may arise in reference to the remedies of law against the sentence. Only the judge of a case can correct any material errors that have crept into a sentence.[69] Only the judge who has issued the sentence which is alleged to be irremediably null is authorized to receive the

---

[65] Canons 1557, § 3; 1569, § 1; 1558.

[66] Canons 247, § 3; 1962.

[67] Roberti, *De Processibus,* I, n. 62.

[68] Canon 1571.

[69] Canon 1878, § 1.

complaint of nullity against that sentence.[70] If the sentence is alleged to be remediably null, then the complaint may be proposed either together with the appeal, or separately and by itself as a separate judicial action. If it is proposed as a separate judicial action, the complaint must be brought before the judge who issued the defective sentence.[71] When the party fears that the judge who pronounced the former sentence is prejudiced, and for that reason justly suspects him, he may demand that another judge, but one of the same court, be substituted in his stead to receive the plaint of nullity.[72]

The judge who issued the sentence or also the judge of appeal is competent to decide the petition of a third party who opposes the sentence.[73] Likewise it is the judge who issued the sentence who is competent to grant the *restitutio in integrum;* however, if the reinstatement in the former position is petitioned because the judge in arriving at the sentence had neglected a precept of law, the reinstatement is granted by the court of appeal.[74]

Only the judge who issued the sentence of contempt of court is competent to reinstate in the right of appeal the person who was guilty of contempt of the court.[75]

With regard to the execution of the sentence, incompetence may arise if anyone other than the ordinary of the place where the sentence was passed, or his delegate, executes the sentence; however, if the local ordinary refuses or neglects to execute the sentence, the judge of the court of appeal is to execute the sentence.[76]

It is evident from the foregoing statements and the laws cited in corroboration of them that a judge may be incompetent in view of the judicial function which he is called upon to perform. The question is whether his incompetence is absolute or relative. The Code nowhere declares an absolute incompetence as deriving from the judicial function that is involved. However, it can be argued that the very nature of functional competence demands that it have

---

[70] Canon 1893.
[71] Canon 1895.
[72] Canons 1615; 1896.
[73] Canon 1899, § 1.
[74] Canon 1906.
[75] Canon 1847.
[76] Canon 1920.

absolute limits. Functional competence is that competence which has to do with the hierarchy of the tribunals, with the series of judicial instances, and with the various activities concerning the same cause. A violation, then, of functional competence would be an essential interference with the hierarchical order of the tribunals, it would nullify the regulations governing the series of judicial instances, and it would render inefficacious the rules regulating the various activities concerning the same cause. Consequently the very nature of competence in respect to the function of the judge demands that it have absolute limits.

Another reason alleged for the absolute character of functional competence is that a violation of it may be a prejudicial attempt against the rights of a party, and by canon 1855, § 1, prejudicial attempts are automatically invalid. Thus if a judge oversteps the bounds of his functional competence, and presumes to adjudicate the irremediable nullity of a sentence that he had not pronounced, he is committing a prejudicial attempt against one of the parties, and thus his decision is *ipso iure* invalid.[77]

In this article the writer has attempted to show that when certain reservation of judicial cases are made by the law in view of the dignity of the persons involved, in consideration of the object of the trial, in consequence of the exclusive transfer of the case to the Holy See, or with advertence to the specific judicial function to be exercised, the reservation is such that all other judges are absolutely incompetent. If such judges decide any of these cases their sentences are irremediably null.[78]

Their jurisdiction cannot be extended with a view that these matters may be covered either at the behest of their own wills or through the consent of the parties. The nullity of their sentence can always (*in perpetuum*) be opposed by means of an exception, and within thirty years from the day of the publication of such an invalid sentence the party concerned has a right to an action to have the sentence declared null by the judge who pronounced it.[79] Moreover, the exception against absolute incompetence can be raised at

---

[77] Cf. canon 1893; Roberti, *De processibus,* I, n. 62.

[78] Canon 1892, 1°.

[79] Canon 1893; 1679.

any moment of the trial.[80] And the established fact of absolute incompetence is to be declared *ex officio* by the judge at whatever stage the trial may have reached, once he recognizes that he is absolutely incompetent.[81]

ARTICLE 4. THE EXCEPTION OF SUSPICION RAISED AGAINST THE JUDGE

A plea of suspicion can be entered against a judge when he has accepted a case for trial in the face of any of the reasons which in law forbid his acceptance of it. Such grounds are the personal interests which a judge may have in a case by reason of the bonds of consanguinity or affinity in any degree of the direct line or in the first or second degree of the collateral line, or by reason of his status of a guardian or a trustee, or of his intimate association or bitter rivalry within one of the parties, or of the likelihood of acquiring gain or of forestalling loss, or finally, in view of the fact that he has in the same matter been an advocate or a procurator for one of the parties.[82]

Canonists quite commonly maintain that this enumeration of causes as grounds for suspicion against the judge should not be regarded as being so complete as to exclude the possibility of other equivalent causes of suspicion. For the defendant has a right, which is based on the demands of the natural law, to defend himself by means of any and all exceptions which are compatible with moral right and the public order.[83]

When one of these causes or an equivalent cause of suspicion has resulted in a raising of the exception of suspicion against the judge, and the incidental question concerning the suspicion has been

---

[80] Canon 1628, § 2.

[81] Wernz-Vidal, *Ius Canonicum,* VI, n. 50.

[82] Canons 1613; 1614.

[83] Cf. canon 1667; Lega-Bartoccetti, *Commentarius,* I, 220, 221; Coronata, *Institutiones,* III, n. 1146; Wernz-Vidal, *Ius Canonicum,* VI, n. 147. However, Roberti (*De Processibus,* I, n. 153, p. 446), states that the list of causes in canon 1613, § 1, presents an all-inclusive enumeration of the causes of suspicion. But this could imply an infringement of the right of defense, and on that score would stand contrary to the natural law.

decided in favor of the litigant who raised the exception, but the judge whose ministry has been lawfully refused nevertheless continues to adjudicate the case, his subsequent judicial acts cannot be said to be invalid, for the present legislation contains no sanction of nullity against such a procedure. The remainder of the trial, though, may be unjust, since the litigant's right to be tried by an impartial judge may have suffered infringement.[84]

The pre-Code controversy concerning the validity of the acts performed by a judge the while the decision regarding the exception of suspicion against him was pending is still undecided. The older commentators were sharply divided on this question.[85]

Among the authors since the promulgation of the Code Roberti[86] favors as the more tenable opinion the one which holds that acts performed by a judge the while there is pending the settlement of the exception of suspicion raised against him are *ipso iure* null. Bartoccetti[87] declares that this opinion seems to be entirely certain and beyond the shadow of a doubt. He argues in the following manner: The nature of the exception of suspicion raised against the judge demands that he suspend his judicial procedure; if he does not, he commits a prejudicial attempt against the party who raised the exception. Since all prejudicial attempts are *ipso iure*

---

[84] Cf. Wernz-Vidal, *Ius Canonicum,* VI, n. 146; Coronata, *Institutiones,* III, n. 1146.

[85] De Luca (*Theatrum Veritatis et Justitiae,* XV, pars I, disc. 3, n. 71) held the acts of a judge to be *ipso iure* invalid if performed during the time while the question regarding the raised exception of suspicion was pending. Vantius (*Tractatus de Nullitatibus Processuum et Sententiarum,* Rub. IX, n. 140) and Maranta (*Speculum Aurem,* pars IV, dist. 16, n. 4) held the same opinion. Cf. also Lega, *De Iudiciis Ecclesiasticis,* Vol. I, lib. 1, n. 570.

On the other hand, Pirhing (*Jus Canonicum,* lib. II, tit. 28, n. 277) claimed that such acts were valid. Engel (*Collegium Universi Juris Canonici,* lib. II, tit. 28, n. 57) explained that such acts were either valid or invalid according as the exception of suspicion was ruled out or sustained. Schmalzgrueber (*Jus Ecclesiasticum Universum,* lib. II, tit. 28, nn. 144-146) and Reiffenstuel (*Jus Canonicum Universum,* lib. II, tit. 28, nn. 326-328) taught that the acts were invalid if the cause of the suspicion was notorious.

[86] *De Processibus,* I, n. 153, p. 449.

[87] *Commentarius,* I, 289.

invalid,[88] the acts of the judge subsequent to the entering of the plea of suspicion are likewise invalid. Vidal (1868-1939)[89] claimed that such acts are indeed valid, but likewise insisted that they are rescissible on the grounds of *dolus* if the exception of suspicion is decided in favor of the party. He reasoned that in the Code there is no explicit statement declaring the nullity of such acts; therefore, in accordance with the norms of canons 15 and 103 such acts are valid but rescissible. Coronata[90] states that such acts are invalid only if the exception of suspicion is verified.

The opinion of Roberti seems to be the better grounded opinion, for it appears to have the stronger juridical support on its side, and it reflects at the same time the Rotal jurisprudence inasmuch as it is held by canonists who are active in the Roman Rota.[91] Consequently one may well regard as invalid the acts that a judge performs the while the solution of the question of suspicion raised against him is still pending.

---

[88] Canons 1854; 1855, § 1.

[89] *Ius Canonicum,* VI, n. 151.

[90] *Institutiones,* III, n. 1146.

[91] Król, *The Defendant in Contentious Trials,* The Catholic University of America Canon Law Studies, n. 146 (Washington, D. C.: The Catholic University of America Press, 1942), p. 109.

CHAPTER III

Nullity Because of the Unlawful Constitution of the Ecclesiastical Tribunal

Article 1. The Judge, the Assessors, and the Auditors

In every diocese for all cases which are not expressly excepted by law, the local ordinary is the judge of the first instance. He may exercise his judiciary power either in person or through others.[1] The law obliges him to appoint an *officialis,* a diocesan judge, to whom is granted ordinary power for judicial affairs. The *officialis* forms part of one and the same tribunal with the bishop of the diocese, but he cannot try cases which the bishop reserves to himself.[2] The *officialis* should be a person other than the vicar general, unless the smallness of the diocese or the limited amount of judicial business makes it preferable to entrust this office to the vicar general.[3] When a vicar general who has not been appointed as the *officialis,* or who has not been delegated as a judge, presumes to exercise judicial power, he acts invalidly in consequence of his absolute lack of judicial jurisdiction.[4]

The bishop of the diocese cannot judicially decide cases involving his own temporal rights and goods, or those which pertain to the bishops mensal fund (*mensa episcopalis*), or those which relate to the diocesan curia. If the bishop judges in matters concerning his own temporal rights or goods, the judicial process is invalid, since it is contrary to the natural law that anyone should be a judge in his own case.[5] Roberti[6] states that, if the ordinary judges the cases that relate to the *mensa episcopalis* or to the diocesan curia,

---

[1] Canon 1572, § 1.
[2] Canon 1573, §§ 1, 2.
[3] Canon 1573, § 1.
[4] Roberti, *De Processibus,* I, n. 96.
[5] Canon 1680, § 1; cf. Roberti, *De Processibus,* I, n. 97, p. 260.
[6] *Loc. cit.*

he acts invalidly if he at the same time presumes to represent these parties, or if, when his ministry in the capacity of a judge has been rightfully refused, he nevertheless proceeds with the case. However, since the law does not provide any sanction of nullity against such a procedure, it seems that the trial may be unjust in its character rather than invalid.[7]

When a judge singly conducts a trial he can employ two assessors or counsellors. These are to be selected from the synodal judges. The assessors are to assist the judge in hearing the case and in reaching a decision; however, they have no powers of jurisdiction. Hence, any acts which they undertake beyond their competence as counsellors are invalid unless they have an appointment from the judge to exercise acts of jurisdiction, provided of course that the judge can delegate such powers to them.[8]

One or several auditors also may be associated with the principal judge in the trial of a case. They are synodal judges or others who help the judge in the process of drawing up the acts of the case.[9] They may perform such acts as the summoning and the examining of witnesses. They may carry out the judicial access and inspection, and they may examine documents.[10]

The law forbids auditors to pronounce the definitive sentence or any sentence which has definitive force. Hence, since whatever powers they have are delegated, the presumption will always be that they do not have jurisdiction to deliver a sentence. Consequently, as long as this presumption cannot be successfully challenged with proof for a provision to the contrary, any definitive sentence which they pronounce is invalid.[11]

ARTICLE 2. THE COLLEGIATE TRIBUNAL

A collegiate tribunal is required under sanction of nullity for the trial of certain judicial cases. Therefore in every diocese, in addition to the appointment of an *officialis,* there is to be constituted a

[7] Cf. canons 11; 1680, § 1.

[8] Canon 1575; Roberti, *De Processibus,* I, n. 102.

[9] Canons 1580; 1582.

[10] Canons 1582; 1773; 1807; 1821, § 2.

[11] Canons 1581; 1582; cf. Roberti, *De Processibus,* I, n. 113, p. 294.

collegiate tribunal for certain kinds of contentious cases and for certain types of criminal trials. Contentious cases involving the bond of sacred ordination or of marriage, or regarding the temporal rights and goods of the cathedral church, and criminal cases involving an irremovable incumbent's deprivation of his ecclesiastical benefice, or the issuing of a condemnatory or a declaratory sentence of excommunication, must be tried by a collegiate tribunal of three judges. Trials in connection with crimes which entail the penalties of deposition, perpetual privation of the clerical garb, or degradation, are reserved to a tribunal of five judges under the sanction of nullity.[12]

It is to be noted that the cases concerning ordination and matrimony which must be committed to a collegiate tribunal of three judges, are those wherein the very bond of sacred orders or of matrimony is impugned. Canon 1576, § 1, 1°, uses the word "bond," rather than the word "validity." Hence, with regard to Sacred Orders, not only the cases which contest the validity of the ordination itself, but also those which concern the obligations that in consequence of the ordination normally bind the subject are reserved to a collegiate tribunal.[13]

Those cases which are reserved by law to a collegiate tribunal are reserved under the sanction of nullity. Hence any sentence, whether it be definitive or interlocutory, which is pronounced by less than the required number of judges in such cases is irremediably null. In this regard every contrary custom is reprobated, and every adverse privilege that had been granted before the Code is revoked.[14]

The local ordinary can commit also other cases to a collegiate tribunal of three or of five judges, and he should do so especially when there is question of cases which seem rather difficult and are

---

[12] Canons 1576, § 1, 1°, 2°; 1892, 1; 205, § 3.

[13] Canons 1576, § 1, 1°; 1993; Lega-Bartoccetti, *Commentarius,* I, 127. Roberti (*De Processibus,* 1, n. 111) considers the cases which involve the obligations that arise from Sacred Orders like the cases which have to do with the juridical effects consequent on matrimony, e.g., the questions regarding the legitimacy of offspring, and he feels that they are not reserved to a collegiate tribunal.

[14] Canons 1576, § 1; 1892, 1°; 1577, § 1; 205, § 3.

of farreaching importance by reason of the circumstances of the time, of the place, of the persons, or of the subject matter of the trial.[15] When the local ordinary commits such cases to a collegiate tribunal, he can permit that one or the other of the judges absent himself from the trial; but if the local ordinary does not make provision for such an absence in the mandate of delegation, and *de facto* not all the members of the collegiate tribunal take part in deciding the issue, the judicial procedure of such a defective tribunal is invalid.[16]

In judicial matters that require the attention of a collegiate tribunal the full number of judges must determine the sentence. However, it is not essential that all the judges are in attendance at each and every act of the trial. Generally all those procedural acts which pertain to the drawing up of the acts of the case and which can be committed to an auditor do not require for their validity the presence of all the judges.[17]

If one of the collegiate judges is incapable of receiving or exercising ecclesiastical jurisdiction, or if he was invalidly appointed to the tribunal, or if he has lost his jurisdiction, then the judicial acts of such a tribunal when it has functioned with this disqualified member are just as invalid as if the court had proceeded without the required number of judges.[18]

ARTICLE 3. THE NOTARY, THE PROMOTER OF JUSTICE, THE DEFENDER OF THE BOND, THE COURIERS, AND THE APPARITORS

The presence of a notary is essential to every judicial process. He performs the office of a secretary, and he is a qualified witness of what takes place in court. The acts of a trial written or signed by him are authoritative documents.[19] If the acts of the case or of the process are not written or at least signed by him they have no

[15] Canon 1576, § 2.

[16] Canon 205, § 3.

[17] Cf. canon 1582; Roberti, *De Processibus,* I, n. 113; Hanssen, *De Sanctione Nullitatis in Processu Canonico,* p. 54; Lega-Bartoccetti, *Commentarius,* I, 134.

[18] Canons 1680, § 1; 205, § 3; 1892, 1°; Hanssen, *loc. cit.*

[19] Canons 1585, § 1; cf. 1813, § 1, 2°, 3°.

value. The wording of canon 1585, § 1, clearly indicates that the notary must be present at the session in order that he may validly write or sign its acts.[20] Roberti states that a judicial tribunal without the services of a notary must be considered as a thing that cannot have existence.[21]

The appointment to the office of notary may be invalid, and as a consequence the appointee cannot function validly in the capacity of notary. For instance, a person who when assigned to a case as a notary is not one of the group of notaries legitimately appointed by the local ordinary cannot validly serve as a notary, since he would be merely a private person and unable to make records that would deserve public credence. This would also be true if one who has been removed or suspended from the office of notary were assigned to a case.[22]

In the exercise of his function the notary is restricted to the territory of the ordinary from whom he has received his appointment. He cannot validly prepare or implement documents elsewhere unless he is aiding his judge who has been exiled from his proper territory or who is impeded from exercising his jurisdiction therein.[23]

The promoter of justice is another official of the diocesan curia in relation to whom nullity may arise in a judicial process. The promoter of justice is a public ecclesiastical official who *ex officio* represents and protects justice and the law. It is his obligation to safeguard the public good and the rights of the ecclesiastical territory of the tribunal to which he is appointed. In cases in which the dispute concerns the bond of sacred orders or the validity of matrimony, the functions of the promoter of justice are exercised by a special official called the defender of the bond.[24]

In trials which require the presence of the promoter of justice, and in those which demand the presence of the defender of the

---

[20] "Cuilibet processui interesse oportet notarium, qui actuarii officio fungatur; adeo ut nulla habeantur acta, si actuarii manu non fuerint exarata, vel saltem ab eo subscripta."

[21] *De Processibus,* I, n. 117.

[22] Canons 1585, § 2; 373; cf. Wernz-Vidal, *Ius Canonicum,* VI, n. 105.

[23] Canons 374, § 2; 1637.

[24] Canon 1586; Wernz-Vidal, *Ius Canonicum,* VI, nn. 111, 119.

bond, the acts of the trial remain devoid of all juridical effect if these officials have not been formally summoned, unless they were actually present even though the summons was omitted.[25] This same invalidity arises if, though summoned or present, the promoter of justice or the defender of the bond has not been validly appointed to his office.[26] The ordinary of the place is to appoint the promoter of justice and the defender of the bond.[27] The vicar general and the *officialis* need special mandates before they can validly appoint these officers of the tribunal.[28]

Other officers of the tribunal are the couriers and the apparitors. The couriers serve to give notice of the judicial acts, and the apparitors serve for the purpose of executing the sentences and the decrees of the judge at his command. These officers do not exercise any jurisdictional power; however, they must be validly appointed if their functions are to have any juridical value. Hence, the unauthorized notification of a judicial summons or the attempted execution of a sentence on the part of a private individual who has no relationship to the tribunal is devoid of juridical effect. A private individual cannot perform such public acts and render them authoritative and worthy of public credence. When an unauthorized person presumes to act as a courier to serve the summons, not only is the summons invalid but the subsequent acts of procedure in the case are null and void.[29]

---

[25] Canons 1587, § 1; 1724.

[26] Roberti, *De Processibus,* I, n. 121, p. 323.

[27] Canon 1589.

[28] Canons 152 and 1432, § 1; Coronata, *Institutiones,* III, n. 1124; Wernz-Vidal, *Ius Canonicum,* VI, n. 114.

[29] Canons 1591; 1593; 1723; cf. Hanssen, *De Sanctione Nullitatis in Processu Canonico,* p. 59.

CHAPTER IV

Nullity Because of the Violation of Certain Procedural Rules

Article 1. The Circumstances of Time and Place Relative to the Trial

A. *Terms of Postponement and the Fatalia Legis*

By *fatalia legis* are meant periods of time during which as fixed by the law certain actions must be performed in order that the right to such actions may not be forfeited. These periods when determined by the procedural law of the Code cannot be extended. They are a matter of public law, for the public good demands that law suits be terminated within a reasonable time. It is to this end that the law has established peremptory periods for the execution of certain acts.[1]

The terms which for the fixing of their duration are committed to the discretion of the judge, and the terms which the law permits the parties to fix by mutual agreement with the approval of the judge, may be prolonged by the judge before their expiration. The extension may be granted at the request of the parties, or also on the initiative of the judge after he has consulted the parties concerning it.[2]

The extension of such judicial or conventional periods of time cannot be effected after the period has lapsed, for that which no longer exists cannot be extended.[3] Once the period of time has lapsed, the adverse party acquires a right to the inhibition of the act in question. If without this party's consent the judge grants a new term for the performance of the act, he commits a prejudicial

---

[1] Canon 1634, § 1; Coronata, *Institutiones,* III, n. 1158; Roberti, *De Processibus,* I, n. 160; for examples of peremptory periods cf. canons 1610, § 3; 1709, § 3; 1688; 1736; 1847; 1881; 1893; 1895.

[2] Canon 1634, § 2; cf. canons 1883; 1676, § 3; 1922, § 3.

[3] Roberti, *loc. cit.*

attempt against him. Consequently the new term which is granted and also the act that is performed are *ipso iure* invalid.[4] If this is true with regard to judicial or conventional terms, it obtains for even greater reason when there is question of the periods of time as fixed by the law, for the adverse party cannot yield his right in connection with them.[5]

The judge cannot, without the consent of the parties, restrict the periods of time which have been granted to them for the obtaining of their rights. For instance, he cannot of his own accord reduce the three days within which the law allows the parties to make known the names of the witnesses.[6] Nor can the judge proceed with the case in relation to the count for the precise determination of which the deferment was granted. Hence a judge cannot proceed with the trial during the period he has allowed an absent party to free himself of the charge of contempt of court.[7] Any interference with the deferment either by the judge or by the adverse party, or any judicial act executed during the time of the deferment and relative to the count for the proper fixing of which the deferment was granted remains void of juridical effect. Such actions are prejudicial attempts against the rights of the litigant and are *ipso iure* invalid.[8]

B. *The Place of the Trial*

The circumstance of place is an important element with regard to the validity of judicial procedure, since territorial limits have been assigned to tribunals for their exercise of judicial powers. The local ordinary and all those who exercise jurisdiction in his name are bound by these territorial limits. Judicial acts illegitimately undertaken outside the territory of a judge are null.[9]

Canon 201, § 2, expressly states that judicial power cannot be

---

[4] Canons 1854; 1855.

[5] Cf. Roberti, *De Processibus,* I, n. 165.

[6] Canon 1764, § 4.

[7] Canon 1729, § 1.

[8] Canons 1854; 1855, § 1; Wernz-Vidal, *Ius Canonicum,* VI, n. 187; Lega-Bartoccetti, *Commentarius,* I, 266; Roberti, *De Processibus,* I, n. 165.

[9] *Infra,* p. 98.

exercised outside one's territory; however, a judge who has been forcibly expelled from his territory, or who is prevented from exercising his jurisdiction there, may exercise his jurisdiction and pronounce sentence outside his territory, but he must inform the local ordinary of the fact that he holds court in his diocese. The omission of this notification of the local ordinary does not however affect the validity of the judicial procedure.[10] Except on such extraordinary occasions when the law extends the jurisdiction of a judge, a judge is absolutely incompetent in judicial affairs when he is outside the territorial limits of his jurisdiction.

The following arguments are adduced in support of this doctrine: 1.) Canon 201, § 2; appears at least equivalently to state the nullity of such acts, for it reads: "*nequit exerceri. . . .*"[11] 2.) Acts which are performed by a judge when outside his territory are invalid for lack of the needed jurisdiction, since his judicial jurisdiction is essentially restricted by territorial limits.[12] 3.) The law which circumscribes the exercise of judicial power within territorial limitations obtained in the pre-Code legislation. It must therefore be interpreted according to the pre-Code authors.[13] Under the Decretal law the exercise of judicial power was limited to the proper territory of the judge.[14] Commentators from the time of the Decretal law until the advent of the Code considered the extra territorial use of judicial power to be invalid.[15] With the exception of Noval (1861-1938),[16] who held the contrary opinion because of the lack of a

[10] Canon 1637; Roberti, *De Processibus,* I, n. 167, p. 485.

[11] Canon 11; Coronata, *Institutiones,* III, n. 1159, nota 4.

[12] "Extra territorium ius dicenti impune non paretur."—D. (2, 1) 20; Roberti, *De Processibus,* I, n. 167.

[13] Canon 6, 2°, 3°.

[14] C. 7, *de officio ordinarii,* I, 16, in VI°; c. 11, *de rescriptis,* I, 3, in VI°; c. un., *de foro competenti,* II, 2, in Clem.

[15] *Glossa Ordinaria* ad c. 7, X, *de officio legati,* I, 30, s. v. *terminos; casus* ad c. un., *de foro competenti,* II, 2, in Clem.; Panormitanus, *Commentaria,* lib. I, tit. 30, c. 7, n. 3; Vantius, *Tractatus de Nullitatibus Processuum et Sententiarum,* rub. IX, nn. 107, 108; Altimarus, *Tractatus de Nullitatibus,* rub. IX, q. 192, nn. 1-8; Schmier, lib. I, tract. 5, c. 8, n. 12; Pichler, lib. II, tit. 2, n. 7; Lega, *De Iudiciis Ecclesiasticis,* Vol. I, lib. I, n. 365; Wernz, *Ius Decretalium,* V, n. 314.

[16] Noval, J., *Commentarium Codicis Iuris Canonici,* Lib. IV, *De Processibus,* Pars 1, *De Iudiciis* (Augustae Taurinorum: Marietti, 1920), n. 232 (hereafter referred to as *De Iudiciis*).

positive sanction of nullity in the law that forbids the extra-territorial use of judicial power, present day commentators maintain that a local judge cannot validly exercise his power outside the territorial limits of his jurisdiction.[17]

With regard to the place of the trial it must be noted also that a bishop can set up a tribunal within his diocese in any place that is not exempt.[18] The exemption referred to is that which directly affects places; hence, there is no doubt that the local ordinary cannot exercise his judicial power in a prelacy or abbacy *nullius*.[19] When the exemption is such that the place is exempt merely by reason of the persons, as is generally the condition relative to the houses of regulars, it is not certain that the exercise of judicial power by the local judge in those places would be invalid. Neither before the Code nor after has there been unanimity on this question.[20] Some authors claim that such judicial acts would be valid, for the place itself is not exempt.[21] Coronata prefers the opinion that the territory

---

[17] Roberti, *De Processibus,* I, n. 167; Felix Cappello, *Summa Iuris Canonici,* Vol. III (editio altera emendata et aucta, Romae: Apud aedes Universitatis Gregorianae, 1940), n. 80; Toso, *Ad Codicem Juris Canonici . . . Commentaria Minora,* Lib. II, tom. 1 (Taurini-Romae: Marietti, 1922), p. 171; Lega-Bartoccetti, *Commentarius,* I, pp. 55, 268, 270; Berutti, *Institutiones Iuris Canonici* (6 vols., Vol. II, Taurini-Romae: Marietti, 1943), II, 321; Eichmann, *Lehrbuch des Kirchenrechts auf Grund des Codex Iuris Canonici* (2. ed., Paderborn: Ferdinand Schöningh, 1926), p. 568; Regatillo, *Institutiones Iuris Canonici* (2 vols., Santander: Sal Terrae, 1941-1942), II, n. 416. Cocchi, *Commentarium in Codicem Iuris Canonici* (8 vols. in 5, Vol. VII, *De Processibus,* 3. ed., Taurinorum Augustae: Marietti, 1940), VII, 106; Vermeersch-Creusen, *Epitome Iuris Canonici* (3 vols., 6. ed., Mechliniae-Romae: H. Dessain, 1937-1946), III, n. 71.

[18] Canon 1636.

[19] Canon 319; Roberti, *De Processibus,* I, n. 167.

[20] Ramos, "De Conditione Saecularium in Domibus Religiosorum," *Commentarium pro Religiosis* (Romae, 1920-1934; ab anno 1935: *Commentarium pro Religiosis et Missionariis*), VI (1925), 28-33 (hereafter cited *CpR* and *CpR.M* respectively).

[21] Roberti, *De Processibus,* I, n. 167, Vermeersch-Creusen, *Epitome,* III, n. 71; Chelodi, *Ius Canonicum de Personis* (3. ed., curavit P. Ciprotti, Trento: Libreria Moderna Editrice, 1942), n. 281. Regatillo, *Institutiones Iuris Canonici,* II, n. 416; Beste, *Introductio in Codicem* (3. ed., Collegeville, Minn.: St. John's Abbey Press, 1946), p. 798.

on which the houses and churches of exempt religious have been erected is altogether separated from the territory of the local bishop.[22] He says that this is more in conformity with pontifical documents.[23] Since neither the arguments for nor the arguments against the validity of the acts induce certitude, it seems reasonable to conclude with Cocchi that a *dubium iuris* is present, and that therefore in accord with the norm of canon 209 such acts would have to be held valid.[24]

ARTICLE 2. THE RECORDING AND THE PRESERVATION OF THE JUDICIAL ACTS

Canonical judicial procedure is for the most part a written procedure. The written court records are instruments of justice. They not only prove the existence of the acts of the case and the acts of the process, but they pertain to the very substance of these acts, for the acts are null if they are not in writing.[25]

The preparatory acts of the trial must be in writing; hence the principal petition is to be presented to the court in an introductory *libellus.* The principal petition may be presented orally when the plaintiff does not know how to write; when for some legitimate reason he is unable to present a written petition; when in the opinion of the judge the case is an easy one and of such minor importance that a written *libellus* would hinder the expeditious handling of the case. When an oral petition is admitted, the judge will order the notary to consign it to writing.[26]

Likewise the summons must be in writing. When no summons is necessary inasmuch as the parties of their own accord have appeared before the judge, the notary must record in the acts that

---

[22] *Institutiones,* I, n. 621, 822, footnote 1.

[23] "Sed quod eorum domus habitae fuerint iuris fictione quasi territoria quaedam ab ipsis dioecesibus avulsa."—Leo XIII, Const. "Romanos Pontifices,"8 Maii, 1881, § 7—*Fontes,* n. 582.

[24] Cocchi, *Commentarium in Codicem Iuris Canonici,* VII, n. 54.

[25] Canons 1585, § 1; 1642, § 1; Roberti, *De Processibus,* I, n. 173; Wernz-Vidal, *Ius Canonicum,* VI, n. 200; Coronata, *Institutiones,* III, n. 1163.

[26] Canons 1706; 1707.

the litigants spontaneously presented themselves in court.[27] The summons is also to be presented to the party in a written form,[28] and the messenger must make a written report of his work in serving the summons. When the summons is served by registered mail, the receipt for the registered letter and the return receipt are to be inserted in the acts of the case.[29] A written account of the joining of issue, namely, of the petition of the plaintiff and of the defendant's reply to it must be inserted in the acts of the case.[30] The judicial decree admitting or rejecting the *libellus,* the mandate of the procurator, and the commission of the advocate must be in writing.[31]

The various proofs that are admitted in the trial are to be recorded; hence the questions submitted to the judge for the interrogation of the parties and their witnesses, as also the responses to these questions, are to be in writing.[32]

The written reports of the experts and specialists and a written account of the judicial access and inspection, must likewise be inserted in the acts of the case.[33]

The notary must record whether the oaths were taken, whether they were dispensed with, or whether they were refused; and generally he must record everything worth noting that happened at the examination of the witnesses.[34] If there is a renouncement of the suit, it too must be made in writing.[35] The defenses, the allegations, and the responses of the parties, of their advocates, of the promoter of justice, and of the defender of the bond must all be consigned to writing.[36] The judges of a collegiate tribunal must present their conclusions regarding the merits of the case in

---

[27] Canons 1712; 1711, § 2.

[28] Canon 1715, § 1.

[29] Canons 1722, §§ 1, 2; 1719.

[30] Canon 1727.

[31] Canons 1709, § 2; 1659, § 1; 1661.

[32] Canons 1745, § 1; 1761, § 1; 1778.

[33] Canons 1802; 1801; 1811, § 1.

[34] Canon 1779.

[35] Canon 1740, § 2.

[36] Canons 1863, §§ 1-2; 1865, § 1.

writing.[37] Finally all the decrees and sentences are to appear in a written form.[38]

Thus it is prescribed that all of the judicial acts be consigned to writing; however, not the entire trial will be void if one or the other act is not recorded. At most that act is null, and the sentence will be invalid only in so far as it depends upon the unrecorded act.[39]

The judicial acts must not only be in writing, but they must be properly signed. The omission of the called for signatures may invalidate these acts. Thus all judicial acts are invalid if they are not signed by the notary.[40] When an individual judicial act is completed, or interrupted, or postponed to another session of the court, it is to be signed by the notary and the judge.[41]

Judicial acts are also to be signed by the persons who execute the acts. For example, the introductory *libellus* is to be signed by the plaintiff or his advocate;[42] a witness must sign the account of his testimony;[43] an expert must sign the statement of his opinion;[44] if the promoter of justice and the defender of the bond are present at the trial, they are to sign the acts that were executed in their presence;[45] the judge or judges and the notary must sign the sentence.[46]

Nullity because of the lack of the required signatures seems to arise solely when the act is not signed by its author and by the notary. The signature of the former is essential to the nature of the act, and the signature of the latter is required under the positive sanction of nullity as enacted in the law.[47]

---

[37] Canon 1871, § 2.

[38] Canons 1872; 1584.

[39] Coronata, *Institutiones,* III, n. 1163; cf. Roberti, *De Processibus,* I, n. 173.

[40] Canon 1585.

[41] Canon 1643, § 2.

[42] Canon 1708, § 3.

[43] Canon 1780, § 2.

[44] Canon 1801, § 1.

[45] S.C. de Sacramentis, instr., *Provida Mater,* 15 aug. 1936; act. 104, § 2—*AAS,* XXVIII (1936), 335.

[46] Canon 1874, § 5.

[47] Canons 1680, § 1; 1585; Roberti, *De Processibus,* I, n. 188.

CHAPTER V

Nullity Because of the Deficient Status of the Litigants

Article 1. The Right of the Principal Litigants to Stand in Judgment

In order that a judicial process exist, there must be, besides the judge, a plaintiff and a defendant, for the judicial trial presupposes a conflict between the rights of at least two parties.[1] If the outcome of the judicial process is to be valid, i.e., if the definitive sentence is to be binding, the plaintiff and the defendant must have the right to stand in judgment (*ius standi in iudicio*).[2]

This expression is comprehensive in meaning. It includes the notion of juridic capacity, along with that of procedural capacity, as well as the notion of a juridic relationship to a determined case. This division of the legal capacity of the parties is generally made by authors. Juridic capacity qualifies a person to be a party in a trial. Procedural capacity enables this party to personally execute procedural acts which produce their proper juridic effect. Juridic relationship to a determined case is the qualification necessary before a certain person can be a plaintiff or a defendant in a definite case.[3]

A. *Juridic Capacity*

In virtue of his juridic capacity a person can be a party in a trial. An essential requisite for the juridic capacity of physical persons in ecclesiastical courts is baptism.[4] Infidels, then, since they enjoy no rights in the Church, are generally denied the right to

---

[1] Coronata, *Institutiones*, III, n. 1168.

[2] Canon 1892, 2°.

[3] Wernz-Vidal, *Ius Canonicum*, VI, n. 203; Roberti, *De Processibus*, I, n. 197; Hanssen, *De Sanctione Nullitatis in Processu Canonico*, p. 82; Król, *The Defendant in Contentious Trials*, p. 66.

[4] Canon 87.

stand in judgment in ecclesiastical courts, at least as plaintiffs. However, this general disqualification cannot infringe upon their natural rights. At times there will exist a sufficient reason to justify the admittance of an unbaptized person as a plaintiff in an ecclesiastical court. Thus in virtue of the privilege of the forum, an infidel may sue a cleric before an ecclesiastical judge. It seeems that the permission of the ordinary of the place where the tribunal is located will give the unbaptized person the right to stand in judgment in such an instance. That the ordinary possesses the power to grant this permission is a deduction from the fact that the Code permits him in exceptional cases to allow non-Catholic advocates and procurators to practice in church courts.[5]

It is to be noted that the Holy Office has reserved to itself the right to permit non-Catholics to act as plaintiffs in matrimonial cases.[6] Authors are generally agreed that if an unbaptized person acted as plaintiff in an ecclesiastical court without any permission he would lack the right to stand in judgment. Consequently the sentence which concludes the trial in his case would be irremediably null.[7]

The generally accepted opinion in reference to the debarment of non-Catholics from acting as plaintiffs in matrimonial cases is that this disqualification is restricted to cases which are introduced before the collegiate tribunal for formal trial, and that non-Catholics are not estopped from acting as petitioners or plaintiffs in summary cases.[8]

---

[5] Canon 1657, § 1; Roberti, *De Processibus,* I, n. 231, p. 637.

[6] S.C.S. Off., 27 ian., 1928; "Utrum in causis matrimonialibus acatholicus, sive baptizatus sive non-baptizatus, actoris partes agere possit. Ad I: Negative, seu standum Codici I.C., praesertim can. 87. Siquidem autem speciales occurrant rationes ad admittendos acatholicos ut actores in huiusmodi causis, recurrendum ad Supreman Sacram Congregationem Sancti Officii in singulis casibus."—*AAS,* XX (1928), 75.

[7] Canons 87; 1646; 1892, 2°; Roberti, *De Processibus,* I, nn. 198, 231; Wernz-Vidal, *Ius Canonicum,* VI, n. 210; Doheny, *Canonical Procedure,* I, 115, 129; Cappello, "De Acatholicorum Incapacitate Agendi in Foro Ecclesiastico," *Miscellanea Vermeersch* (2 vols., Romae: Pontificia Universita Gregoriana, 1935), I, 400.

[8] Petrus Gasparri, *Tractatus Canonicus de Matrimonio* (ed. nova ad mentem Codicis I.C., 2 vols., Typis Polyglottis Vaticanis, 1932), II, n. 1260,

If the unbaptized person is the defendant in a case in which an ecclesiastical tribunal is competent, and the trial is held and the sentence is pronounced, the sentence cannot be attacked on the score that the defendant lacked the right to stand in judgment, for the Code requires no special qualification for a defendant, but makes the absolute statement that a defendant who is lawfully summoned has the obligation to respond.[9]

The right of baptized non-Catholics to stand in judgment in church courts will be considered below under the heading, Legitimation to Act in a Certain Case.[10]

Besides physical persons also moral persons may have juridic capacity according to the ecclesiastical law.[11] Within the Church moral entities obtain their legal personality either from the Canon law, or from a special concession of the competent ecclesiastical authority through a formal decree, which establishes such moral persons whether collegiate or non-collegiate for a religious or a charitable purpose.[12] The lack of moral personality is not a cause of judicial nullity, since there is a well-founded opinion that even merely private pious associations have juridic capacity, so that they can sue and be sued in ecclesiastical courts.[13]

The Code does not expressly consider juridic capacity in its legislation on the right to stand in judgment. It rather presupposes it and directs its canons to procedural capacity.

B. *Procedural Capacity*

By procedural capacity is meant that right in virtue of which a party in a trial can personally execute procedural acts which pro-

---

p. 293; cf. the private reply of the Holy Office, April 20, 1931, to the Bishop of Harrisburg.—Bouscaren, *The Canon Law Digest* (2 vols., Milwaukee: The Bruce Publishing Company, 1934-1943), II, 252.

[9] Canon 1647.

[10] *Infra*, p. 132.

[11] Canons 100, §3; 1552, § 2, 1°; 1649; 1653; cf. Kilcullen, *The Collegiate Moral Person as Party Litigant*, The Catholic University of America Canon Law Studies, n. 251 (Washington, D. C.: The Catholic University of America Press, 1947), p. 59.

[12] Canon 100, § 1.

[13] Roberti, *De Processibus*, I, n. 198, p. 545.

duce their proper juridic effects.[14] Procedural capacity is sometimes referred to as *legitimatio ad processum.*[15] It is a qualification which persons sometimes lack even though they enjoy juridic capacity. The first group of such persons comprises those who are denied procedural capacity in consequence of their lack of the requisite age.

1. Minors

According to the norm of canon 1648, § 1, minors lack procedural capacity. Consequently if a minor is either plaintiff or defendant in a trial, the sentence is irremediably null.[16] The cases of minors can be validly pleaded or defended by their parents or guardians. The parents or guardians must actually represent the minor in the trial. They do not merely assist their charges or authorize them to act.[17] If the judge thinks that the rights of the child are in conflict with the rights of the parents or the guardians, or that they live at so great a distance from the parents or guardians that the latter cannot at all or only with great difficulty represent their charges in court, he is to appoint a guardian *ad litem* for the minor. Once the judge has appointed a guardian *ad litem,* the representation of the minors by their parents or former guardians seems to be invalid, for they have been replaced in this capacity and no longer enjoy any title which would give them the right to represent their former charges in court.[18]

In spiritual cases and in cases connected with spiritual affairs, minors over fourteen years of age enjoy full procedural capacity. In the same affairs those under fourteen years of age who enjoy the use of reason may act and respond in court without the consent of their parents or guardians, but they must act through a proxy designated by themselves and approved by the ordinary, or through a guardian assigned to them by the ordinary.[19] Once minors are

[14] Król, *The Defendant in Contentious Trials,* p. 66.

[15] Roberti, *De Processibus,* I, n. 197.

[16] Canon 1892, 2°.

[17] Canon 1648, § 1; Król, *The Defendant in Contentious Trials,* p. 69.

[18] Canons 1648, § 2; 1892, 2°; Roberti, *ibid.,* n. 201, p. 554; Hanssen, *De Sanctione Nullitatis in Processu Canonico,* p. 77.

[19] Canon 1648, § 3.

vindicated in their right to independence in causes involving spiritual matters, any further representation by their parents or guardians is invalid, for the minor's incapacity, the final cause for their functioning as representatives, has come to an end. This is also true in causes involving other than spiritual matters when minors have attained their majority and signify that they wish to handle their own judicial affairs.[20]

2. The Insane, Prodigals, and Weak-minded Persons

Persons who lack the use of reason do not have procedural capacity. Among these are infants and the insane.[21] Infants can be validly represented in court by their parents or guardians, the insane by their curators.[22] As in the case of minors, if there is a conflict between the rights of the persons who lack the use of reason and the rights of those who represent them, the judge must appoint a *curator ad litem.* After this appointment the former representatives function invalidly.[23]

Prodigals and weak-minded persons have a limited procedural capacity.[24] They can appear in court personally only to answer for their own delicts, or at the order of the judge. Hence they may always appear in criminal trials to defend themselves, but in contentious cases they may stand in judgment only at the order of the judge. In all other cases they must sue and be sued through a curator.[25] The ecclesiastical judge may, but he is not obliged to, follow the opinion of civil authorities concerning the prodigality or mental weakness of the litigants.[26] However, curators assigned to

[20] Roberti, *De Processibus,* I, n. 201, p. 554; Hanssen, *op. cit.*, p. 77.

[21] Canons 1648, § 1; 88, § 3.

[22] A guardian is given to a person who is incapable of acting legally because of deficiency in his age; a curator is given to one who is incapable of acting legally because of some mental deficiency.—Coronata, *Institutiones,* III, n. 1174; Wernz-Vidal, *Ius Canonicum,* VI, n. 207.

[23] Canon 1648, § 2; Roberti, *De Processibus,* I, n. 201, p. 554.

[24] Prodigals are those who have been deprived of the administration of their goods because of their spendthrift habits.—Woywod, *A Practical Commentary on the Code of Canon Law* (Revised and enlarged edition by Callistus Smith, 2 vols., New York: Joseph F. Wagner, Inc., 1948), II, 229.

[25] Canon 1650.

[26] Coronata, *Institutiones,* III, n. 1176, Roberti, *De Processibus,* I, n. 202.

prodigals and weak-minded persons by civil authority can be admitted to the ecclesiastical forum only with the consent of the ward's ordinary, who may, if he deems it prudent, appoint another curator for the canonical trial.[27]

Who are to be considered prodigals or weak-minded persons is not determined in the Code.[28] The preliminary drafts of the Code indicate that more specific legislation on this point had been contemplated. There was raised the question whether a sentence is required before one can be deprived of the administration of his goods. *Ojetti* (1862-1932) suggested that it be left to the judge to decide who are prodigals (*"ii quos iudex prodigos aut interdicendos iudicaverit"*). Another opinion left the matter of determining who are prodigals to the physical examination of experts. Another suggestion was that a special process be constituted to determine prodigals under the title *"De Interdictione Personarum."* However, the opinion which favored a general canon was the one that was finally adopted and incorporated in the Code as canon 1650.[29]

Certainly, then, a judicial sentence is not absolutely required in order that a person be considered weak-minded or a spendthrift. The ordinary can by an act of his voluntary administration deprive such a person of the administration of his affairs.[30] However, if the pronouncement that he is such is contested, he cannot be deprived of the administration of his goods until his incapacity or disqualification has been proved by means of a formal judicial process.[31]

A preliminary draft of the Code indicated that the ordinary was by means of a decree to assign a curator to a person who was not sufficiently capable of protecting his own rights. The ordinary could make this assignment only after he had interviewed the ward, his intimate acquaintances, and experts, and after he had examined whatever pertinent documents there were.[32]

---

[27] Canon 1651.

[28] Coronata, *Institutiones,* III, n. 1176.

[29] Roberti, *Codicis Iuris Canonici Schemata,* Lib. IV, *De Processibus* (Romae: Typis Polyglottis Vaticanis, 1940), Schema D. Can. 127, § 1, not. 2 (hereafter referred to as *Schemata*).

[30] Roberti, *De Processibus,* I, n. 58, p. 164.

[31] Coronata, *Institutiones,* III, n. 1176; Roberti, *De Processibus,* I, n. 202, p. 556.

[32] Roberti, *Schemata,* D., Can. 127, § 2.

The Pontifical Commission for the Authentic Interpretation of the Code had declared that a regular trial is not required, but that rather a simple decree of the ordinary upon a prudent inquiry suffices for the assigning of a guardian to those who are destitute of the use of reason or who are weak-minded. This is the interpretation which the Commission vindicated for the statement contained in canon 1651, § 1.[33]

It is to be noted that prodigals and weak-minded persons lose their procedural capacity from the moment that they are pronounced incapable of administering their own affairs. Before this pronouncement they have the right to stand in judgment; however, the process is invalid if they in fact lack the use of the powers of reason.[34]

When persons who have been declared prodigals or weak-minded sue or are sued without representation in court, the sentence which concludes the trial will be irremediably null. They can validly appear in court only by order of the judge or to answer for their own delicts.[35] It seems that the sentence is also invalid if their representative in court is an unauthorized person. Such a representative in the trial would not have any title whereby he acquired the right to stand in judgment.[36]

The parents have a natural right to represent their children in the trial. Any other curators have to be approved by the ordinary, for even a curator who is appointed by the civil authority cannot be admitted by the ecclesiastical judge without the consent of the ordinary of the ward.[37] When there is a conflict between the rights of the ward and the rights of the duly appointed curator, or when the curator is a considerable distance away from the court, it seems that the provision of canon 1648, § 2, can be followed. This canon provides for the same contingencies with reference to those who lack the use of reason. It empowers the judge to appoint a curator *ad litem.*

---

[33] 25 ian., 1943—*AAS,* XXXV (1943), 58 (hereafter this Commission is designated with the symbols *PCI*).

[34] Roberti, *De Processibus,* I, n. 202, p. 558; Hanssen, *De Sanctione Nullitatis in Processu Canonico,* p. 77; Canons 1648, § 1; 1892, 2°.

[35] Canons 1892, 2°; 1650.

[36] Cf. canon 1892, 2°.

[37] Canon 1651, § 1.

3. Religious

Without the consent of their superiors religious do not have the right to stand in judgment either as plaintiffs or as defendants.[38] This law applies to all religious, regardless of whether they have simple or solemn vows. It is to be noted that novices do not lose their procedural capacity since they are not religious properly so called, although they enjoy the benefits and privileges of religious.[39] In certain cases, though, the law permits the individual religious to retain his procedural capacity. A religious can appear in court without the consent of his superior in order to vindicate the rights that he has acquired from his institute through his religious profession. For instance, he may appear in court to prove his right to proper sustenance, or his right to share in the benefits and privileges of his community.[40]

A religious who is dwelling lawfully outside the inclosure of his monastery can appear in court without the consent of his superior when the defense of his rights becomes urgent. Thus, if a religious is away from his institute for the sake of studies or because of ill health and then becomes deprived of his possessions by force or stealth, he has an absolute right to appear in court to institute an action to regain his possessions.[41] By this same token a religious

---

[38] Canon 1652; Coronata, *Institutiones,* III, n. 1177.

[39] Canons 488, 7; 567, § 3; Roberti, *De Processibus,* I, n. 207, p. 574; Lega-Bartoccetti, *Commentarius,* I, 316, n. 7; Coronata (*Institutiones,* III, n. 1177) says that religious of simple vows can be validly sued without the consent of their superiors in cases concerning property over which they retain the right of ownership. However, this distinction between religious of solemn vows and those of simple vows is not in accord with canon 1652.

Canon 1652 refers only to individual religious and not to the convent, province or order as such. Moreover, the law concerns them as religious, and not as rectors or administrators of moral persons. The religious in such a position is acting not as a religious in his own name, but in the name of the moral person.—Noval, *De Iudiciis,* n. 257.

Persons who lead a community life without being bound by the usual three vows are not religious properly so called, and therefore do not come under the disqualification of canon 1652. Cf. canons 673, § 1; and 19.

[40] Canon 1651, 1°; Roberti, *De Processibus,* I, n. 207.

[41] Canon 1652, 2°; Lega-Bartoccetti, *Commentarius,* I, 317; Roberti, *De Processibus,* I, n. 207, p. 576.

who has been created a cardinal, or has been promoted to the episcopal dignity, or has become entrusted with the care of a parish, has procedural capacity for protecting the rights which he acquires by these positions.[42] The law also grants to an individual religious the right to institute a judicial denunciation of his superior. Thus a religious can inform the promoter of justice that his superior is wasting the goods of the community, and he can supply him with proofs of the superior's extravagant administration.[43]

If a religious makes a contract without any permission from his superiors, he, and not the religious organization, is responsible for the terms of that contract.[44] However, in order that the religious may proceed validly in a trial relative to such a contract he needs the consent of his superior. The fact that the religious is personally responsible for the terms of the contract in no way changes the procedural regulation that he requires the consent of his superiors in order to validly stand in judgment. If such a religious is sued without the consent of his superior even a sentence that is unfavorable to the religious is null in virtue of his procedural incapacity.[45]

All authors concur in the opinion that religious must respond for their own delicts, and that they can be sued in contentious trials for the damage arising from such delicts whether or not the superior's consent is obtained.[46]

---

[42] Coronata, *Institutiones,* III, n. 1177; Roberti, *loc. cit.;* Lega-Bartoccetti, *op. cit.,* I, 318.

[43] Canon 1653, 3°; Lega-Bartoccetti, *loc. cit.*

[44] Canon 536, §§ 2, 3.

[45] Canons 1652; 1892, § 2; Noval, *De Iudiciis,* n. 257; cf. Król, *The Defendant in Contentious Trials,* p. 71; Roberti, *De Processibus,* I, n. 207, p. 576; Wernz-Vidal (*Ius Canonicum,* VI) stated that a religious of simple vows can be sued without the consent of his superior for a debt which he unlawfully contracted. However, canon 1652 hardly allows this distinction, since ordinarily when the consent of the superior is lacking it denies procedural capacity to a religious whether he is the plaintiff or the defendant in the case. It would seem that the religious superior has no option in the matter of withholding his consent when the plaintiff has no other resort in law than a lawsuit. The plaintiff's right to invoke a suit against the religious overrides any and every right a superior may have to withhold from the religious every right of standing in court. Cf. Roberti, *loc. cit.*

[46] Thus Lega-Bartoccetti: "Quamvis hic canon 1652 non expresse dicat at subintelligitur. quippe est omnino extra controversiam atque certis ex prin-

It seems that an apostate or fugitive religious also needs the consent of his superior in order that he may validly stand in judgment, for canon 1652, § 2, grants procedural capacity solely to religious who are lawfully outside the enclosure of the monastery. Hence, if an apostate or fugitive religious is sued without the consent of his superior and an unfavorable sentence is pronounced against him, he can lodge a plaint of nullity against this sentence, since he did not have the right to appear in court. If such is the case, the apostate or fugitive religious profits by his own misconduct. To obviate such a miscarriage of justice and to preclude the possibility of an irremediably null sentence in such a case, Król suggests that, if the permission of the religious superior cannot be obtained, then the consent of the local ordinary should be obtained. He argues that by canon 616, § 1, regulars who are unlawfully absent from their houses forfeit the privilege of exemption, and in virtue of canon 500, § 1, such religious appear to be subject to the local ordinary. Consequently the ordinary's consent would give such religious the right to stand in judgment.[47]

The legislation on the procedural capacity of religious has important practical consequences, since by canon 1892, 2°, a judicial sentence is irremediably null if one of the parties does not have the right to stand in judgment.[48]

4. Moral Persons

Moral persons, whether they be collegiate or non-collegiate, by their very nature are incapable of standing in judgment themselves.[49] They must sue and be sued through their rector or administrator.[50] In case there is a conflict between the rights of the

---

cipiis fluens, nempe ipsum religiosum respondere debere nedum de delictis sed etiam civilibus, quos vocant, derivantibus ex delicto: can. 2210, n. 2. Asseruimus autem haec non esse aliena a canonis 1652 praescripto."—*Commentarius,* I, 316; cf. also Roberti, *De Processibus,* I, n. 207, p. 577; Coronata, *Institutiones,* III, n. 1177, p. 84; Wernz-Vidal, *Ius Canonicum,* VI, n. 206, p. 174.

[47] *The Defendant in Contentious Trials,* pp. 72-73.

[48] Lega-Bartoccetti, *Commentarius,* I, 319.

[49] In Canon law moral persons are considered as minors.—can. 100, § 3.

[50] Canon 1649.

moral person and the rights of its rector or administrator, the ordinary will appoint a procurator to represent the moral person. Thus, if a lawsuit exists between a moral person and a close relative of its administrator, the administrator may very well be suspected of partiality towards his relative. In such a case the ordinary must appoint a procurator to represent the moral person.[51]

Although the immediate rector or administrator of a moral person is preferably the one who is to represent that person in court, the local ordinary or his delegate, in virtue of his capacity either as supervisory administrator or as extraordinary administrator, can in default of the ordinary administrator litigate in the name of the moral persons that come under his jurisdiction.[52]

Since the unauthorized representation of moral persons in court results in irremediable nullity to the sentence in the case,[53] it will be necessary to consider the procedural norms which govern the representation of moral persons in ecclesiastical trials.[54] Moral persons are either non-collegiate or collegiate in character. Collegiate moral persons may be secular or religious. The discussion which follows will have to do with a.) non-collegiate moral persons, b.) secular or non-religious moral persons, c.) religious moral persons.[55]

a.) *Non-collegiate Moral Persons*

The local ordinary can validly represent in court the interests of the cathedral church and of the episcopal mensal fund.[56] In order to act licitly the ordinary must, in accordance with the amount of money involved in the case, consult or secure the consent either of

---

[51] Canon 1649; cf. Lega-Bartoccetti, *Commentarius,* I, 307.

[52] Canon 1653, § 5.

[53] Canon 1892, 2° ; Roberti, *De Processibus,* I, n. 204, p. 564; Lega-Bartoccetti, *Commentarius,* I, 308.

[54] Canon 1653.

[55] Cf. canon 99, Roberti, *De Processibus,* I, nn. 203, 204.

[56] The *mensa episcopalis* comprises whatever is necessary for the temporal sustenance of the ordinary and the members of the diocesan curia.—Coronata, *Institutiones,* III, n. 1175, p. 87, footnote 3; Noval, *De Iudiciis,* n. 258.

the cathedral chapter (diocesan consultors) or of the board of administrators.[57]

The procedural capacity of other non-collegiate moral persons is provided for in that they can validly stand in court through the agency of their rectors or administrators.[58] Hence a benefice is validly represented by its beneficiary. In order that the beneficiary act licitly he must abide by the precept of canon 1526, which demands that he obtain the written permission of the local ordinary as a preliminary to entering upon a suit; in urgent cases the permission of the rural dean suffices, but he in turn must inform the local ordinary of his action.[59]

In like manner the representative of the collegiate chapter has the right to stand in judgment for the collegiate church, the proper rector for a church that is *sui iuris,* a pastor for his parish.[60] and the rector of the seminary for the seminary.[61] Benefices which belong to moral persons are not represented in court by their actual incumbents, but by those who are qualified to represent the moral person to which they are united.[62] Educational institutions, if they are moral persons in their own right, are represented in court by their rectors or presidents.[63] Other pious institutions, such as hospitals, orphanages and the like, are represented in court according to the particular statutes of their foundation or charter.[64]

Ordinarily administrators of moral persons need the consent or advice of others who are connected with the institutions which they represent, especially for the more important matters and questions

---

[57] Canon 1653, § 1. It is to be noted that while canon 1653, § 1, refers to canon 1532, §§ 2, 3, it does not provide that the same formalities as are stated therein for the alienation of ecclesiastical goods are required also for the valid representation in court of the interests of the cathedral or of the episcopal mensal funds.—Roberti, *De Processibus,* I, n. 205. Lega-Bartoccetti, *Commentarius,* I, 321; Coronata, *Institutiones,* III, n. 1175.

[58] Canon 1659.

[59] Canon 1653, § 2.

[60] Wernz-Vidal, *Ius Canonicum,* VI, n. 209, p. 179; cf. canon 1892, 2°

[61] Roberti, *De Processibus,* I, n. 205, p. 567 sqq.

[62] Canons 1653, § 3; 609, § 1; 415, §§ 1, 3, 3°.

[63] Roberti, *ibid.,* p. 570.

[64] Canon 1489, § 3.

of extraordinary administration.[65] Roberti feels that this consent or advice is necessary for the valid entering into a litigation.[66] However, the tenor of canon 1653, which is the controlling one in this question, indicates that this consent or advice is necessary only for the licit undertaking of the litigation.[67] This was the pre-Code interpretation of the law.[68]

Roberti demands also that in certain instances, e.g., for entering into a suit involving the interests of a church that is *sui iuris,* the permission of the ordinary be obtained for the validity of the action; however, canon 1653, § 2, explicitly states this permission is required only for the licitness of the suit.[69]

The unauthorized representation in court of a non-collegiate moral person entails the irremediable nullity of the sentence which terminates the suit. It should be noted, though, that the invalid alienation of ecclesiastical goods can be contested by the person who alienated them, by his superior, by the successor of either in office, and by any cleric who is assigned to the church which has sustained the loss.[70]

b.) *Secular Collegiate Moral Persons*

Chapters, sodalities, and other collegiate bodies or moral persons[71] can be validly represented in court by their prelates and

---

[65] Canons 105; 1653, § 3.

[66] Roberti, *De Processibus,* I, n. 205, p. 566.

[67] Canon 1653, § 1; cf. Hanssen, *De Sanctione Nullitatis in Processu Canonico,* p. 79.

[68] Schmalzgrueber, lib. II, tit. 1, n. 39; Reiffenstuel, lib. II, tit. 1, nn. 169, 172-178.

[69] Roberti (*loc. cit.*) bases his opinion on canon 1527, which demands the written consent of the ordinary for validity in all extraordinary acts of administration; however, if this provision be extended to include acts of litigation, the preceding canon in the Code would be superfluous, for canon 1526 expressly requires an administrator to secure the permission of the ordinary before entering into a lawsuit, and canon 1653, § 2, states that this permission is required for the lawfulness of such an act.

[70] Canons 1892, 2°; 1534, § 2.

[71] Associations which have ecclesiastical approval and even merely private associations can be validly represented in court even though they are not moral persons, for they are capable of obtaining spiritual favors, particularly

superiors; however, a prelate or a superior cannot validly act in court in the name of his community or organization except with its consent according to its statutes.[72] Prelates are clerics, either secular or religious, who have ordinary jurisdiction in the external forum.[73] The superiors of the chapter referred to are the immediate superiors, for example, the deans. The superiors of sodalities and other corporations are either the rectors or the administrators of these moral collegiate persons.[74] These superiors, then, cannot stand in judgment in the name of the chapter, of the sodality, or of any other collegiate moral person without the consent of the community as called for by its statutes.[75] The statutes here referred to are based on the franchise or on the certificate of incorporation or on the decree of erection issued by the competent ordinary.[76]

It seems that prelates and superiors need the consent of the community only if this precaution is prescribed by the statutes, for the canon reads: *"sine eiusdem consensu ad normam statutorum."* However, some canonists say that the consent is always required unless the statutes provide otherwise.[77]

The better opinion is that the consent of the corporation is not required unless the statutes expressly call for it,[78] since in the preliminary drafts of the Code there was a clause which stated that the consent of the community was required unless the statutes pro-

---

indulgences. Since the Code recognizes that such an association can possess rights, it is argued that it can be represented in court for the protection or vindication of those rights. Cf. canons 708; 686, § 1; Roberti, *De Processibus,* I, n. 198; Maroto, *Institutiones Iuris Canonici* (2 vols., Matriti, 1918-1919), I, n. 459, c.; S.R.R. *Treviren,* Diffamationis, 15 maii, 1913, coram R.P.D. Seraphino Many—*AAS,* V (1913), 286.

72 Canon 1653, § 3.

73 Canon 110.

74 Noval, *De Iudiciis,* n. 258, p. 162.

75 Canon 1653, § 3.

76 Kilcullen, *The Collegiate Moral Person as Party Litigant,* p. 102.

77 Coronata, *Institutiones,* III, n. 1175, p. 82; Noval, *De Iudiciis,* n. 258, p. 163; Vermeersch-Creusen, *Epitome,* III, n. 78; Lega-Bartoccetti, *Commentarius,* I, 323.

78 Roberti, *De Processibus,* I, n. 204, p. 561; De Meester, *Juris Canonici et Juris Canonico—Civilis Compendium* (nova editio, 3 vols. in 4, Brugis: Desclée De Brouver, 1921-1928), Tom. III, Pars. I, n. 1558, p. 36; Kilcullen, *The Collegiate Moral Person as Party Litigant,* p. 103; Król, *The Defendant in Contentious Trials,* p. 75.

vided otherwise, but this clause was deleted and does not appear in the present Code.[79]

It is to be noted that if the statutes do require the superior to obtain the consent of the community in order to represent the community in court, then this consent, in virtue of canon 1653, § 3, is necessary for the validity of the representation, since the canon states: *"stare in iudicio nequeunt"*; hence the absence of such a required consent would result in the nullity of the trial. The particular statutes cannot decree that the consent is necessary only for the licitness of the representation, for such a provision would be contrary to the law of the Code. The Code leaves the community free to determine by its particular statutes whether or not the consent is required, but once the statutes prescribe its necessity, canon 1653, § 3, makes it necessary for the validity of the representation.[80] When the consent of the community is required by its statutes and the superior acts contrary to the vote of the community then he acts invalidly.[81]

Judicial nullity, then, arises in relation to secular collegiate moral persons when they appear in court through anyone but their lawful representative, or when their representative has not obtained the consent of the community if the statutes require it, or when representative who is obliged to obtain the consent of the community acts contrary to its expressed will.[82]

c.) *Religious Moral Persons*

The procedural capacity of religious communities is not regulated by the provisions made for the moral persons already dis-

[79] ". . . stare in iudicio nequeunt, nomine respectivae communitatis, absque eius consensu, salvis constitutionibus et statutis particularibus legitime recognitis quae aliud caveant."—Roberti, *Schemata,* G, can. 113, § 3; cf. also *Schemata,* F, can. 115, § 1; D, can. 130, § 1; C, can. 105, § 1.

[80] Cf. Roberti, *De Processibus,* I, n. 204, p. 561; Król, *op. cit.,* p. 76. Coronata, *Institutiones,* III, n. 1175, note 4; Vermeersch-Creusen, *Epitome,* III, n. 78. Noval maintained that the consent was not required for the validity of the trial if the statutes required it merely for the lawfulness of the action.—*De Iudiciis,* n. 258. However, this is contrary to the evident meaning of canon 1653, § 3, and to the opinion of the majority of the commentators.

[81] Canon 105, 1°.

[82] Canons 1892, 2°; 1653, § 3; 105, 1°.

cussed in this dissertation. There is in canon 1653, § 6, a special precept that controls their right to stand in judgment. They can be represented in court by their superiors, but only according to the constitutions or statutes of the community. The superiors include those persons who as members of religious institutes of men and women, or of particular houses and provinces of such institutes, enjoy the particular power to safeguard the rights of the corporation and to administer its temporalities.[83]

Superiors who represent a religious community may need the consent of the community or the consent of an administrative board before entering upon litigation. Sometimes, however, this consent is unnecessary, and at most the advice of some councilors must be heard. No general rule can be given, since the procedure that is to be followed depends on the particular constitutions of the institute: *"Superiores religiosi nequeunt nomine suae communitatis stare in iudicio, nisi ad normam constitutionum."*[84]

While the unauthorized representation in court of a moral person, whether it be collegiate or non-collegiate, will in general entail an irremediable nullity of the sentence, this eventuality may be obviated by means of a subsequent ratification of the preceding invalid acts by the lawful representative or superior. This subsequent ratification cannot be carried out if the adverse party has taken exception to the incapacity of the unauthorized representative, or if the court *ex officio* at any time during any period of the trial rules against the unauthorized representation, or if the court in an action initiated within thirty years of the publication of the invalid sentence has set aside that sentence. Ratification cannot be effected in the event of these contingencies, for then the matter has ceased to be dependent solely on the will of the principal.[85]

C. *Legitimation to Act in a Certain Case*

The legitimation to act as a litigant in a determined contentious or criminal case is an extrinsic quality. It is the qualification that is

---

[83] Noval, *De Iudiciis,* n. 261; Coronata, *Institutiones,* III, n. 1175, p. 82; Lega-Bartoccetti, *Commentarius,* I, 326, n. 8.

[84] Canon 1653, § 6; Lega-Bartoccetti, *loc. cit.;* cf. Roberti, *De Processibus,* I, n. 204, p. 563.

[85] Canons 1892, 2°; 1893; Roberti, *De Processibus,* I, n. 204, p. 564.

necessary before a determined person can be a plaintiff or a defendant in a definite case. It is possible, though, that a person may possess passive legitimation, i.e., the ability to be a defendant, and at the same time not enjoy active legitimation, i.e., the right to be a plaintiff. Legitimation is only explained as the juridic relationship of a person to a determined judicial suit. Unless that juridic relationship exists, a person is barred from litigating either personally or by proxy in a determined trial. The lack of this required legitimation does not always invalidate the sentence. Legitimation differs from procedural capacity in that procedural capacity is a prerequisite for any judicial process, while *legitimatio ad causam* is a prerequisite for a particular lawsuit.[86] The meaning of this qualification is perhaps best grasped from a consideration of the canons which control it.

Thus canon 1971, § 1, declares that only the consorts are qualified to impugn the validity of their marriage or to plead for a separation. They alone have the juridic relationship to the particular judicial action. No one else can be the plaintiff in a matrimonial case, except, of course, the promoter of justice in case wherein the impediment is by nature public.[87] The spouses themselves are debarred from impugning the validity of their marriage if they are the cause of the impediment.[88] However, this disqualification of the guilty consort is not of such a nature that the sentence which concluded the trial in which the debarment was not enforced would be vitiated with the irremediable nullity mentioned in canon 1892, 2°.[89]

The right to impugn the validity of sacred ordination rests solely with the cleric and the ordinary to whom the cleric is subject or in whose diocese he was ordained. Moreover, only the cleric can petition the Holy See for a declaration of the nullity of the obligations that normally attach to the receptance of Sacred Orders.[90] Only the

---

[86] Wernz-Vidal, *Ius Canonicum,* VI, n. 203, note 16; Hanssen, *De Sanctione Nullitatis in Processu Canonico,* p. 82. Roberti, *De Processibus,* I, n. 231.

[87] Cf. Roberti, *De Processibus,* I, n. 231, p. 638.

[88] Canon 1971, § 1.

[89] *PCI,* 4 ian. 1946—*AAS,* XXXVIII (1946), 162.

[90] Canon 1994.

promoter of justice to the exclusion of all others can institute a criminal action in ecclesiastical courts.[91]

The law is not clear concerning the personal right to stand in judgment on the part of *excommunicati vitandi* and of all such persons in whose excommunication a declaratory or a condemnatory sentence has intervened. They can institute an action personally for the sake of impugning the justice or the legality of their excommunication. They can act by proxy in order to avert anything else that may prove prejudicial to their spiritual welfare. In all other cases they are not to be admitted to institute a suit in ecclesiastical courts.[92]

Some canonists interpret canon 1654, § 1, to mean that in all other cases such excommunicated persons do not have the right to stand in judgment, and consequently the judicial procedure in which they act as plaintiffs is invalid.[93] This opinion appears to be too rigorous and seems unwarranted in the text of the law, for canon 1654, § 1, states no more than that such excommunicated persons are to be repelled from acting as plaintiffs. Hence no positive sanction of nullity is attached to the precept which prohibits them from initiating a lawsuit. Consequently they cannot be said to lack absolutely the right to stand in judgment.[94]

There has been no certain change, then, from the earlier law in this regard, for the Decretal legislation explicitly stated that the judicial acts executed by excommunicated persons were not invalid.[95] Moreover, in the preliminary drafts of the Code Cardinal Lega proposed that the appropriate canon state that *excommunicati vitandi* can never validly act as plaintiffs.[96] This proposal was not

---

[91] Canon 1934.

[92] Canon 1654, § 1.

[93] ". . . qui non habent personam standi in iudicio ad agendum seu tamquam actores."—Wernz-Vidal, *Ius Canonicum,* VI, n. 206. "Defectus legitimationis activae ad causam cum agitur de excommunicatis vitandis aut toleratis quorum excommunicatio inflicta vel declarata est per sententiam vel per modum praecepti, est absolutus; ideoque processus et sententia nullitate laborant ob defectum personae standi in iudicio."—Roberti, *De Processibus,* I, n. 208, p. 581. Cf. also Hanssen, *op. cit.,* pp. 83, 84.

[94] Canon 1680, § 1; cf. Noval, *De Iudiciis,* n. 250.

[95] C. I, *de exceptionibus,* II, 12, in VI°.

[96] ". . . numquam valide agere possunt."—Roberti, *Schemata,* C. can. 106, § 1, note 8.

incorporated in the Code. Hence it can be argued that the legislator did not wish to state that the judicial acts of such excommunicated persons are invalid. Among the commentators since the publication of the Code this opinion is held by Lega-Bartoccetti.[97]

Excommunicated persons who are *tolerati* and who are not sentenced can initiate a suit unless they are to be repelled by reason of a judicial exception which has been invoked in view of their excommunication. Canon 1628, § 3, gives the defendant the right to delay the trial by invoking such an exception when the plaintiff is an excommunicate. It seems that the exception can be raised also to break the contumacy of the excommunicated person and to avert any danger of perversion that may exist for the faithful through associating with one who is excommunicated.[98] Even though, after such an exception is raised, the judge proceeds further with the case, the subsequent judicial acts are not invalid, since the plaintiff does not lack the right to stand in judgment.[99]

All excommunicated persons are bound to appear in court when they are summoned, lest through a justified absence from court they derive profit from their own malice, and lest by their non-appearance they miss the opportunity of a defense in the suit which is brought against them.[100]

Baptized non-Catholics, viz., apostates, heretics, and schismatics, are not directly denied by the Code the right to stand in judgment. Some authors exclude them on the grounds that they are excommunicated.[101] However, as has been demonstrated,[102] excommunicated persons cannot be said to lack the right to stand in judgment in the sense that, if one of them is a party in a trial, the sentence which concludes that trial will be invalid.

---

[97] *Commentarius,* I, 331, n. 9.

[98] Cf. Coronata, *Institutiones,* III, n. 1156, p. 64, n. 1.

[99] Cf. *supra,* p. 130.

[100] Canon 1646; Roberti, *De Processibus,* I, n. 208, p. 580; Lega-Bartoccetti, *Commentarius,* I, 329; Noval, *De Iudiciis,* n. 264.

[101] Canon 2314, § 1, 1°; Albertus Blat, *Commentarium Textus Codicis Iuris Canonici, Liber IV, De Processibus* (Romae: Collegio Angelico, 1927), n. 122 (hereafter cited *De Processibus*); Charles Augustine, *A Commentary on the New Code of Canon Law* (8 vols., Vol. VII, 3. ed., St. Louis, Mo.: B. Herder & Co., 1930), VII, 106 (hereafter cited *Commentary*).

[102] *Supra,* p. 130.

If one looks to the interpretation of the pre-Code law for light on this question, one finds that non-Catholics were not absolutely debarred from taking part in ecclesiastical trials. Ordinarily in criminal cases non-Catholics, i.e., pagans, Jews, heretics, and schismatics, were not to be admitted as plaintiffs or accusers against Catholics, and especially not against clerics. In so far, however, as they were subject to the jurisdiction of the Church they could be summoned as defendants in criminal cases which the ecclesiastical courts were competent to decide. In contentious cases, though non-Catholics ordinarily were not to be admitted as plaintiffs, there were some instances in which they could and had to be admitted, e.g., in cases involving a mixed marriage.[103]

Because of the silence of the Code and in view of the interpretation of the earlier law, it cannot be concluded that non-Catholics absolutely lack the right to stand in judgment in ecclesiastical courts. Certainly they can stand as defendants, for the present law states without qualification that a defendant who is lawfully summoned must respond.[104]

There are not lacking modern commentators who admit that non-Catholics have some right to appear in church courts.[105]

The Sacred Congregation of the Holy Office, however, declared that non-Catholics,[106] whether baptized or unbaptized are unable to act as plaintiffs in matrimonial cases, and that the provisions of canon 87 are to be observed. If there are special reasons for admitting non-Catholics as plaintiffs in such cases, recourse must be had in each case to the Supreme Sacred Congregation of the Holy Office.[107] Directly and immediately this response refers to the right to impugn the validity of a marriage, but in virtue of its allusion to

---

[103] Wernz, *Ius Decretalium,* V, n. 169.

[104] Canon 1646.

[105] Wernz-Vidal, *Ius Canonicum,* VI, n. 210; Coronata, *Institutiones,* III, n. 1173; Cappello, "De Acatholicorum Incapacitate Agendi in Foro Ecclesiastico," *Miscellanea Vermeersch* (2 vols., Roma: Pontificia Universitá Gregoriana, 1935), I, 398.

[106] The term non-Catholics in this decree includes apostates from the faith. Cf. S.C.S. Off., 15 ian. 1940—*AAS,* XXXII (1940), 52.

[107] S.C.S. Off., resp. 27 ian. 1928—*AAS,* XX (1928), 75.

canon 87[108] it can be interpreted to refer to any type of judicial petition. Hence, ordinarily non-Catholics do not have legitimation to act as plaintiffs in the ecclesiastical forum.

Whether they are debarred under sanction of invalidity to the process is another question. Some authors feel that if a non-Catholic acted as a plaintiff in a church court without the permission of the Holy Office the process and the sentence would be invalid.[109] However, it is not immediately evident that this is the meaning of the debarment of non-Catholics. The word *"possit"* was used in the question submitted to the Holy See in 1928, and the word *"nequent"* appears in article 35, § 3, of the Instruction on Matrimonial Procedure of 1936, which states this debarment, but this is not sufficient justification to interpret the provision as the equivalent statement of an invalidating law.[110]

It seems prudent to refrain from declaring that this debarment carries with it the sanction of invalidity in the light of a recent response of the Pontifical Commission for the Interpretation of the Code in answer to an analogous question. The Commission declared that the estoppel of a guilty consort to impugn a marriage does not imply that the incapacity to stand in judgment is of such a nature that the sentence is vitiated with the irremediable nullity mentioned in canon 1892, 2°, in the event that this prohibition is not observed.[111]

Legitimation to act in a definite case is one of the requisite qualifications a litigant must enjoy before entering into a lawsuit; however, not all the laws which control legitimation are invalidating laws. Some of the canons which govern this qualification are such;[112] others, as has been pointed out, are not.[113]

---

[108] ". . . quia obstat obex ecclesiasticae communionis vinculum impediens." Cf. Roberti, *De Processibus*, I, n. 231, p. 637; Cappello, "De Acatholicorum Incapacitate Agendi in Foro Ecclesiastico," *Miscellanea Vermeersch*, I, 400.

[109] Doheny, Canonical Procedure, I, 115; Cappello, "De Acatholicorum Incapacitate Agendi in Foro Ecclesiastico," *Miscellanea Vermeersch*, I, 400.

[110] Canon 11; S.C.S. Off., resp. 27 ian. 1928—*AAS*, XX (1928), 75. S.C. de Sacramentis, instr. *Provida Mater*, Art. 35, § 3—*AAS*, XXVIII (1936), 321.

[111] *PCI*, 4 ian. 1946—*AAS*, XXXVIII (1946), 162.

[112] Canons 1971, § 1; 1994; 1934.

[113] Canon 1654; S.C. de Sacramentis, inst. *Provida Mater*, Art. 35, § 3—*AAS*, XXVIII (1936), 321; *PCI*, 4 ian. 1946—*AAS*, XXXVIII (1946), 162.

Hence the conclusion of Hanssen that the lack of the requisite legitimation to act in a case renders the trial invalid is too broad a statement and one which is not always verified.[114]

ARTICLE 2. UNAUTHORIZED PROCURATORS

Parties in a lawsuit in ecclesiastical courts are given the option of conducting the trial personally or of being represented before the tribunal by means of a procurator. The latter method in most instances is to be preferred.[115] A judicial procurator, then, is a person legitimately appointed, and admitted by the ecclesiastical court for the purpose of representing one of the principal parties in a lawsuit that is being prosecuted before that tribunal.[116]

Only one procurator should be appointed to represent a litigant in a lawsuit.[117] Canon law, however, recognizes certain situations in which more than one procurator may be necessary. Nevertheless, only one procurator can function at a time in an ecclesiastical trial. The litigant, for a just cause, may appoint several procurators, but he must authorize them *in solidum,* thus making the principle of exclusive precedence operative. The procurator who precedes the others by actually assuming the representation of his principal excludes the others from validly acting for him.[118] Moreover, a procurator cannot validly substitute another to take his place, unless he has been expressly granted the power to do so. If he does, the substitute will not be in possession of a legitimate mandate. Consequently the sentence will be vitiated with the irremediable nullity mentioned in canon 1892, 3°.[119]

The all important and all controlling factor for the validity of a judicial process carried on by a procurator is the special mandate which precisely grants him the power of attorney for judicial

---

[114] *De Sanctione Nullitatis in Processu Canonico,* p. 85.

[115] Canon 1655, § 3; Roberti, *De Processibus,* I, n. 212, p. 589.

[116] Cf. Hogan, *Judicial Advocates and Procurators,* The Catholic University of America Canon Law Studies, n. 133 (Washington, D. C.: The Catholic University of America Press, 1941), p. 4.

[117] Canon 1656, § 1.

[118] Canon 1656, § 2; 1892, 3°. Cf. Roberti, *De Processibus,* I, n. 212.

[119] Canon 1656, § 1.

affairs. Judicial activity in a trial in the absence of a legitimate mandate results in a sentence that is vitiated with irremediable nullity.[120] Not only is the mandate essential to the validity of the trial, but of equal importance is the fact that the mandate must be legitimate. In every detail it must fulfill the requirements of the law. A mandate will be illegitimate, then, in consequence of any disqualification in the principal or in the person who is appointed as procurator. This illegitimacy may arise, too, in consideration of the very nature of the mandate, or in view of the fact of its expiration.[121]

A mandate is illegitimate with reference to the principal litigant when it is given by one who is not a party in the suit, or when it is given by one who does not enjoy juridic or procedural capacity.[122] It is illegitimate in relation to the person who is appointed as procurator when that person lacks juridic or procedural capacity; hence a minor or one who lacks the use of reason cannot be granted the power of attorney to carry on a lawsuit.[123]

A mandate is invalid in consideration of its very nature when it does not contain the name of the principal litigant, or when it does not specifically designate the person upon whom it purports to bestow the power of attorney.[124] Moreover, the mandate must be a specific commission for judicial affairs. A general mandate for all transactions is no longer sufficient for the valid conduct of judicial matters.[125] Coronata points out that a general mandate, provided that it also contains express authorization for judicial affairs, complies with the legal requirement of a special mandate.[126]

---

120 Canons 1659, § 1; 1892, 3°; Roberti, *De Processibus,* I, n. 214, p. 597; Lega-Bartoccetti, *Commentarius,* I, 341; Cappello, *Summa Iuris Canonici,* III, 145; Wernz-Vidal, *Ius Canonicum,* VI, n. 239; Hanssen, *op. cit.*, p. 86.

121 Cf. Hanssen, *op. cit.,* p. 86.

122 Roberti, *De Processibus,* I, n. 214, p. 597; cf. *supra,* pp. 105, 108.

123 Roberti, *loc. cit.;* Hanssen, *op. cit.,* p. 87; cf. *supra,* pp. 109, 110.

124 Canon 1680, § 1; Hanssen, *op. cit.,* p. 88.

125 Canon 1659, § 1 ". . . speciale mandatum ad lites." Roberti, *De Processibus,* I, n. 214, p. 592; Coronata, *Institutiones,* III, n. 1185; Noval, *De Iudiciis,* p. 180; Cappello, *Summa Iuris Canonici,* III, 145; Cocchi, *Commentarium in Codicem I.C.,* Lib. IV, p. 134. Cf. Reiffenstuel, lib. I, tit. 38, n. 86.

126 *Institutiones,* III, n. 1185.

The specification of the mandate need not be determined with reference to each particular process. All that is required for validity is that the document grant the power to act in judicial affairs. The mandate may be special for one, for several, or for all lawsuits in which the principal is a party. Normally a procurator is appointed for a particular suit before a diocesan tribunal.[127] Roberti remarks that there is nothing to prevent a party from designating an agent for certain procedural acts or even for a single act.[128]

If the mandate of the procurator is not drawn up in writing, it fails to meet the requirements of the law. Consequently an unwritten mandate will occasion judicial nullity. The present legislation abolishes the possibility of a valid representation in court in consequence of an oral, a tacit, or a presumed authorization. To be valid the judicial mandate must be in writing.[129] An express written mandate is always required, even when in view of an accorded gratuitous patronage the litigant is favored with a procurator designated by the court.[130] Tacit acquiescence with the court's choice is insufficient in view of the Code's stringent insistence that the mandate be expressly delivered in writing. Even when a procurator is deemed necessary by the court, he must receive his commission from the litigant in the ordinary manner prescribed by law.[131]

The written judicial mandate is illegitimate if it is not deposited with the chancery of the tribunal either in its original form or in an authenticated copy. The presentation of the mandate to the court is necessary before the judge can admit the procurator to the trial. The mandate may be introduced separately as a distinct

---

[127] Lega-Bartoccetti, *Commentarius,* I, 341.

[128] Roberti, *De Processibus,* I, n. 212, p. 588.

[129] Canon 1659, § 1 ". . . mandatum ad lites scriptum." Roberti, *De Processibus,* I, n. 214, p. 595; Cappello, *Summa Iuris Canonici,* III, 145; Noval, *De Iudiciis,* p. 180; Hanssen, *op. cit.,* p. 88.

[130] Cf. canon 1916.

[131] Cf. canon 1655, § 3. Lega-Bartoccetti (*Commentarius,* II, 1021) advance the opinion that a tacit designation suffices in the case of gratuitous patronage, but this view is unwarranted by the present legislation. Cf. Hogan *Judicial Advocates and Procurators,* p. 106.

document, or it may be embodied in or attached to the introductory *libellus*.[132]

There is a directive in the Code to the effect that a notation of the granted mandate be incorporated also in the official summons of the defendant. It seems that this order is sufficiently complied with if the defendant is informed in the summons of the fact that the plaintiff proposes to act through a particular procurator.[133] The validity of the mandate does not seem to hinge on the fact of its notation in the summons, for the mandate is already executed, so that the failure to include a notation of it in the summons as well appears not to vitiate the mandate itself in such a manner as to make it illegitimate in the invalidating sense of canon 1893, 3°.[134]

The judicial mandate is also illegitimate when its authenticity is not evident from the personally executed signature of the principal. Even when the mandate is drawn up by the hand of another it must be signed personally by the one granting the power of attorney.[135] The general law of the Code does not require an official authentication of the principal's signature, for the Code does not demand that he sign the mandate in the presence of his pastor or of a notary, or in the presence of the tribunal.[136] However, with regard to this point when a presumptively existing bond of matrimony is being impugned, the Instruction *Provida Mater* of 1936 supplements the Code. Article 49, § 1, demands that the signature of the principal be certified by the pastor or by the curia. This certification, at least with reference to matrimonial procedure, seems to be required with such rigor that its absence would render the mandate illegitimate in the invalidating sense of canon 1892, 3°.[137]

---

[132] Canon 1659, § 1: ". . . mandatum . . . apud tribunal deposuerit." Cf. canons 1708; 1819; S.C. de Sacramentis, instr. *Provida Mater,* Art. 49, § 1—*AAS,* XXVIII (1936), 324; Wernz-Vidal, *Ius Canonicum,* VI, n. 239; Roberti, *De Processibus,* I, n. 214, p. 595; Noval, *De Iudiciis,* n. 280.

[133] Canon 1659, § 1: ". . . mandatum . . . etiam in calce ipsius citationis." Cf. Coronata, *Institiones,* III, n. 1185, p. 92, note 1.

[134] Hogan, *op. cit.,* p. 115, note 17.

[135] Canon 1659, § 1: ". . . mandatum . . . mandantis subscriptione munitum." Noval, *De Iudiciis,* p. 180.

[136] Roberti, *De Processibus,* I, n. 214, p. 596.

[137] *AAS,* XXVIII (1936), 324; cf. Hogan, *op. cit.,* pp. 105, 106; Roberti, *De Processibus,* I, n. 214, p. 596.

In the event that the principal is unable to write, the mandate will be illegitimate and accordingly will occasion the nullity of the sentence if certain legal provisions are not followed for the purpose of insuring its authenticity in the absence of the principal's certified signature.[138] The provisions of canon 1659, § 2, explicitly state what procedure is to be followed when one is intellectually incapable of writing; however, there can be no doubt that this procedure becomes applicable also in the face of a physical incapacity on the part of the one who issues the mandate.[139] In the first place, the written document must contain mention of the fact that the principal is unable to affix his personal signature to the mandate. Secondly, the genuineness of the mandate must be guaranteed through the signature of the pastor or through the signature of an ecclesiastical notary of the diocesan curia. In the absence of such a signature on the part of the pastor or of the notary the mandate must be signed by two capable witnesses.[140]

The mandate granting the power of attorney will also be illegitimate if it does not definitely specify the details of place and time with regard to its execution. The document must contain the address, at least the name of the city wherein it is signed, and it must clearly indicate the day, the month, and the year in which the principal affixed his signature thereto. All these details relate to the validity of the judicial process.[141]

If the procurator executes acts which exceed the powers entrusted to him through the terms of his mandate, his acts are invalid.[142] The mandate which he has received as empowering him to conduct the lawsuit does not commission him to perform certain extraordinary judicial acts for which the law demands a specific mandate.[143] This specific mandate must meet all the requirements already set down as necessary for the valid constitution of a legiti-

---

[138] Canon 1892, 3°.

[139] Cf. Hogan, *op. cit.*, p. 108.

[140] Canon 1659, § 2; Blat, *De Processibus*, n. 137, p. 168.

[141] Canon 1659, § 1: ". . . locum, diem, mensem et annum referens." Blat, *De Processibus*, p. 167; cf. canon 1892, 3°.

[142] Canon 203, § 1.

[143] Canon 1662.

mate mandate to conduct a lawsuit.[144] The procurator who lacks such a specific mandate cannot validly renounce or relinquish the trial, the hearing, or any judicial acts legally connected with the process.[145] Nor can he validly negotiate a friendly settlement of the issue (*transactio*) without a special authorization.[146]

An ordinary procurator is incapable of entering into an agreement with the other litigant through which a lawsuit involving a clear, certain claim is terminated or foregone through a friendly remittance of the claim as a donation out of pure liberality.[147] The procurator who is unsupported by a special mandate is disqualified from validly effecting a settlement of his client's claim by way of compromise through arbitration.[148] Such a procurator cannot give or require of the other party judicial oaths. It does not matter whether the question is one of a supplementary oath, of an estimatory oath, or of a decisory oath. A special mandate is always required for the validity of the oaths taken either by the procurator or by the adverse party upon the request of the procurator.[149]

The procurator does not need a special mandate to prosecute the appeal. At least his lack of special authorization will not be a ground for the nullity of such an appeal, since there is a doubt of law about the necessity of a special mandate in such an event. The better opinion is that no special commission is required, for the Code confers upon the procurator, when there is no restraint on the part of his client, the right and the duty to make the appeal; hence, the Code makes no distinction between filing the appeal and prosecuting it.[150]

---

[144] Hogan, *op. cit.*, p. 112.

[145] Canon 1662; cf. canon 1740.

[146] Canon 1662; cf. canon 1925. "A transaction is a contract between the parties wherein a supposed or doubtful legal claim is settled by peaceful agreement for a mutual consideration, thereby ending the lawsuit pending, or obviating a process about to be initiated."—Hogan, *op. cit.*, p. 113.

[147] Canon 1662.

[148] Canon 1662; cf. canons 1929-1931.

[149] Canon 1662; cf. canons 1829-1836.

[150] Vermeersch-Creusen, *Epitome*, III, 41; Lega-Bartoccetti, *Commentarius*, I, 349; Hogan, *op. cit.*, pp. 162 ff.; Roberti, *De Processibus*, I, n. 214. p. 594; Connolly, *Appeals*, The Catholic University of America Canon Law Studies,

In reference to matrimonial processes, which must be tried in two instances, the Instruction of 1936 provides that the procurator needs special authorization to represent his client in the court of the second instance.[151]

A controversy among the authors exists also concerning the necessity of a special mandate before a procurator can lodge a formal complaint of nullity against the sentence. Consequently it seems that without any special authorization the procurator is free to petition for this remedy against the sentence when there is reason for his invoking it.[152]

The opinion that no special mandate is needed seems to be the better one, for the procurator *ad litem* is empowered to execute any and all such related acts for which the law does not demand a special mandate. Nowhere does the law indirectly intimate that a specific authorization is necessary before the procurator can use this remedy.[153]

A procurator who lacks a specific commission cannot perform any of those acts for which the law demands a specific mandate. Just what further judicial acts are forbidden to the ordinary procurator is of no small importance, since there is always the sanction of nullity to be considered in the event of an illegitimate or nonexistent mandate.[154]

On the grounds that the same requirement existed in the pre-Code law, authors are generally agreed that a special mandate is

---

n. 79 (Washington, D. C.: The Catholic University of America, 1932), pp. 154, 155. The opinion that a special mandate is required for a prosecution of the appeal is favored by Hanssen (*De Sanctione Nullitatis in Processu Canonico,* p. 89) and by Eichmann (*Das Prozessrecht, des Codex Iuris Canonici* [Paderborn, 1921], pp. 97, 98).

[151] Art. 52, § 2—*AAS,* XXVIII (1936), 325.

[152] Canon 15. Noval (*De Iudiciis,* p. 182) and Roberti, *De Processibus,* I, n. 214, p. 594) demand a special mandate before the procurator can lodge the complaint of nullity against the sentence. The contrary opinion is held by Coronata (*Institutiones,* III, n. 1420), Muñiz (*Procedimientos Eclesiásticos* [2. ed., 3 vols., Seville: Lib. de Sobrino de Izquierdo, 1926], III, 479), Wernz-Vidal (*Ius Canonicum,* VI, n. 617) and Doheny (*Canonical Procedure,* I, 347).

[153] Cf. Wernz-Vidal, *Ius Canonicum,* VI, p. 617

[154] Lega-Bartoccetti, *Commentarius,* I, 344.

necessary before the procurator can petition for the extraordinary remedy of the *restitutio in integrum*.[155] Some commentators also state that the existence of a particular or of a general custom would prove sufficient to render obligatory a special mandate for certain judicial acts.[156]

The civil law of a particular region may be the source of an obligation requiring specific authorization before a procurator can execute certain judicial acts in an ecclesiastical tribunal, for a mandate reflects a form of contract,[157] and it is a principle of canon law that the civil law governing contracts must be observed in the ecclesiastical forum unless it is contrary to the Divine law, or unless Canon law rules otherwise.[158]

Judicial nullity arises relative to the expiration of the agent's mandate when the procurator attempts to represent his client after his commission has come to an end.[159] Ordinarily, once the hearing of the trial has been completed and the appeal has been prosecuted, the prosecutor is incapable of any further valid representation of his client. Thus he would be unable to petition for the *restitutio in integrum* for the reason that his commission has expired.[160] Moreover, judicial acts which are performed by a procurator subsequent to his receiving an authentic notification of his removal from the case are invalid. If the issue of the trial has already been joined, the removal is ineffective until the knowledge of it has been conveyed to the judge and to the adverse party.[161]

---

[155] Cf. canons 1905-1907; Lega-Bartoccetti, *Commentarius,* I, 345; Coronata, *Institutiones,* III, n. 1426; Roberti, *De Processibus,* I, n. 214, p. 594; Noval, *De Iudiciis,* p. 182; Doheny, *Canonical Procedure,* I, 114; cf. Reiffenstuel, lib. I, tit. 38, n. 103.

[156] Blat, *De Processibus,* p. 169; Noval, *De Iudiciis,* p. 182; Cocchi, *Commentarium in Codicem Iuris Canonici,* VII, 134.

[157] In American law agency is ordinarily, but not necessarily, a contractual relationship. The relation between the principal and his agent may arise from a contract or from a gratuitous agreement.—*American Jurisprudence,* by the editorial staff of the publishers, Vol. II (Rochester, New York: The Lawyers Cooperative Publishing Company, 1936), Agency, §§ 3, 23.

[158] Canon 1529; Noval, *De Iudiciis,* p. 182.

[159] Roberti, *De Processibus,* I, n. 214, p. 597.

[160] Cf. Roberti, *De Processibus,* I, n. 214, pp. 594, 596; Hanssen, *De Sanctione Nullitatis in Processu Canonico,* p. 88.

[161] Canon 1664, § 1.

The mandate of the procurator is considered to expire also when before the issue is joined the principal dies, or changes his status, or loses the office by reason of which he acted in the case. If death or one of these other eventualities comes to the principal after the issue has been joined, the trial is suspended; however, when the lawful heir resumes the lawsuit, the procurator may continue to function lawfully in virtue of his original authorization. When death intervenes after the closing of the case, the judge may proceed to deliver the definitive sentence to the procurator.[162]

A procurator would certainly act invalidly if he attempted to represent his client after he had effectively resigned his commission. It is to be noted that the commission does not cease to exist until the resignation has been accepted by the client, and, if the issue has been joined, until the court and the adverse party have been notified of this fact.[163]

When a procurator is repulsed from the trial by means of an official ruling of the judge, any further actions on his part will hardly be considered efficacious by that judge. If the debarred procurator is again admitted to the case, his former capacity to execute valid judicial acts revives so that he need not obtain another mandate from his client. The ruling of the judge did no more than suspend his activity, for the procurator has his authorization to act from the litigant, and not from the judge.[164]

As has been shown in the foregoing pages, the procurator's mandate is a vulnerable point for the intrusion of judicial nullity into a trial. If the procurator lacks a mandate or one that is legitimate, his acts, and the acts which the judge and the adverse party execute in relation to him, are invalid. Once the definitive sentence is pronounced in such a trial the court is absolutely incompetent to validate the sentence, and the passage of time cannot effect its convalidation, since it is irremediably null.[165]

---

[162] Canon 1733; Roberti, *De Processibus,* I, n. 214, p. 597; Hanssen, *op. cit.,* p. 89.

[163] Cf. canon 207, § 1; Roberti, *De Processibus,* I, n. 214, p. 597; Hanssen, *op. cit.,* p. 89; Hogan, *Judicial Advocates and Procurators,* p. 127.

[164] Cf. Hanssen, *op. cit.,* p. 88.

[165] Canons 1892, 3°; 1659.

However, prior to the definitive sentence the principal can ratify the acts that were invalid in consequence of the lack of a legitimate mandate on the part of his agent, unless the adverse party has raised an exception against them. Ratification does not imply a presumed mandate, it rather establishes a legal fiction whereby the legitimate mandate is considered to have existed from the start of the trial. On the other hand, a ratification cannot be effected if the principal had no power to appoint a procurator or personally did not have the capacity for executing the acts at the time when the acts were attempted. In such a case the legitimate mandate could hardly be considered to exist from the start of the trial. Ratification must be made according to the rules of canon 1659, and it must be effected prior to the pronouncement of the sentence, for the will of a private litigant is powerless to convalidate the sentence, which is an act of public law.[166]

---

[166] Lega-Bartoccetti, *Commentarius,* I, 346; Hanssen, *op. cit.,* p. 90. Cf. Reg. 10, R.J., in VI°: "Ratihabitionem retrotrahi, et mandato non est dubium comparari."

CHAPTER VI

Nullity in the Course of the Trial

Article 1. The Bill of Complaint

A lawsuit is initiated through the offering of a bill of complaint by a plaintiff to a competent judge. This bill is to state the object of the controversy and to implore the service of the judge in order that its author may obtain the rights that are claimed.[1] The bill of complaint is so necessary according to the view of Lega-Bartoccetti that a trial which begins without the presentation of the introductory *libellus* is null.[2] This statement is too absolute. While it was true in the pre-Code law, yet[3] in view of the acknowledged reluctance of the present law to invoke the sanction of nullity[4] it cannot be said that in every instance the omission of the bill of complaint will nullify the judicial proceedings, for the claim of the plaintiff may be sufficiently determined in the summons or in the joining of issue, so that the trial will not be lacking any essential element.[5]

It is difficult to conceive a case in which a trial is invalid with reference to the requirement of the bill of complaint. The present law attaches no sanction of nullity to this requirement, and it is not so essential to a trial that without it a trial cannot exist. If the

---

[1] Canon 1706.

[2] "Quare nullum est iudicium incoeptum absque libelli oblatione, etsi partes in omissionem consenserint."—*Commentarius,* II, 513. Cf. also Blat, *De Processibus,* n. 200; Kealy, *The Introductory Libellus in Church Court Procedure,* The Catholic University of America Canon Law Studies, n. 108 (Washington, D. C.: The Catholic University of America, 1937), 22.

[3] C. 1, X, *de libelli oblatione,* II, 3; Schmalzgrueber, lib. II, tit. 3, n. 11; Bouix, *Tractatus de Judiciis Ecclesiasticis,* II, 143.

[4] Cf. canon 1680.

[5] Canons 1708, 1715, § 1; 1726-1728; Wernz-Vidal, *Ius Canonicum,* VI, nn. 370, 400; Hanssen, *op. cit.,* 94; Roberti, *De Processibus,* Vol. I (Romae: Apud Aedes Facultatis Iuridicae ad S. Apollinaris, 1926), nn. 297, 301.

bill of complaint is omitted entirely, and the judge knows the petition of the plaintiff from some other source, so that he is able to issue a legitimate summons, then the summons can make up for the absence of the bill of complaint. When there is neither a bill of complaint nor a legitimate summons, but the parties of their own accord appear in court, the want of a bill of complaint is compensated for by the petition of the plaintiff which is expressed in the joining of issue.[6] Moreover, nowhere in the law is it mentioned that deficiences in the form and contents of the bill of complaint are among those faults which vitiate the subsequent judicial acts and the ensuing sentence with remediable or irremediable nullity. Hence, a consideration of the essential requirements of the introductory petition is not within the scope of this dissertation. The heaviest legal discrimination that may be visited upon a *libellus* which does not meet the requirements of the law is the fact that it may be rejected by the judge as inept.[7]

ARTICLE 2. THE JUDICIAL SUMMONS

Inasmuch as the defendant has a natural right to defend himself, he is entitled to receive a legitimate summons and notice of the trial.[8] This summons is so necessary that, if it is omitted, or if it lacks the elements required by law, or if it is not lawfully served, the subsequent acts of the process and the ensuing sentence are remediably null.[9] Even the summons seems superfluous or in cases wherein it is impossible to consign it to the defendant personally, a

---

[6] Canons 1715, § 1; 1711, § 2; 1726-1728; S.R.R., *Querelae Nullitatis Matrimonii,* coram R.P.D. Andrea Jullien, 8 febr., 1936 dec. XII, n. 6—*Sacrae Romanae Rotae Decisiones Seu Sententiae* (ab anno 1909) (Romae: Typis Vaticanis, 1912-), XXVIII (1936), 119 (hereafter to be cited as *Decisiones*).

[7] Canon 1709, 2; cf. Kealy, *op. cit.,* p. 39.

[8] Canon 1711, § 1; Lega-Bartoccetti, *Commentarius,* II, 525: Coronata, *Institutiones,* III, n. 1240; Wernz-Vidal, *Ius Canonicum,* VI, n. 384.

[9] Canons 1723; 1894, 1°; S.R.R., *Matriten.* (Nullitatis Actorum et Sententiae) 3 iul. 1933, coram R.P.D. Francisco Parrillo, dec. XLVIII, n. 2—*Decisiones,* XXV (1933), 421; S.R.R. *Viennen.* (Quaerelae Nullitatis et Nullitatis Matrimonii), 22 maii, 1937, coram R.P.D. Alberto Canestri, dec. XXXV, n. 2—*Decisiones,* XXIX (1937), 354.

summons at least by edict is required for the validity of the judicial process.[10]

Wernz-Vidal stated that an edictal summons suffices when a crime is notorious. For instance, a defendant who has been apprehended in a flagrant violation of the law need not be informed that legal action is going to be taken against him, for he already knows this.[11] This opinion does not quite harmonize with the norms of the Code. The edictal summons is a substitute method for informing the defendant of the trial. It is to be used when his whereabouts cannot be determined. Moreover, the defendant is entitled to the favors which the positive law grants him. Therefore he has a right to be personally informed that he has been named the defendant in a court action, especially so that he may know the time and the place that have been determined for his appearance in court.[12]

The defendant may anticipate and thereby obviate the necessity of a summons by appearing in court of his own accord. By his voluntary appearance in court the judicial process will possess the same validity that it would have enjoyed if the formal summons had been issued.[13] His appearance in court in response to an invalid summons can also be presumed to be voluntary, and thus he supplies for the invalidity of the summons. If he does not respond of his own accord but only because he erroneously considers the summons to be valid, then in virtue of the sanction of nullity attached to the regulations for a legitimate summons the subsequent acts of the process are invalid. In this case neither of the prescribed alternate situations are verified. He has not received a lawful summons, and he has also not appeared voluntarily.[14]

---

[10] Canon 1720.

[11] *Ius Canonicum,* VI, n. 384.

[12] Canons 1720, § 1; Coronata, (*Institutiones,* III, n. 1240) states that the summons is unnecessary when the crime of the defendant is notorious since in such an instance the right of defense is entirely useless. This opinion is hardly in accord with the natural law presumption that a man is innocent until he has been proved guilty, and with his natural right to defend himself.

[13] Canon 1711, § 2.

[14] Canons 1711, § 2; 1723; 1725. Wernz-Vidal (*op. cit.,* VI, n. 393, nota 48) state: "Si reus ad citationem nullam compareat, quasi ea teneretur ob ignoratam citationis nullitatem, videretur dicendum omnes actus processuales posteriores infici nullitatis vitio, cum can. 1711, 1723 exigant validam cita-

Since the requirements of the Code for a legitimate summons are prescribed under sanction of remediable nullity from the viewpoint of the summons itself in relation to the subsequent acts of procedure and the resulting sentence, a detailed consideration of the canonical regulations which govern the contents and the service of the judicial summons is in order.[15]

The summons can be issued only by the judge, for it is an act that involves the exercise of judicial jurisdiction;[16] hence the canonical procedure does not countenance the practice of some civil codes in accordance with which the plaintiff issues the summons. By the same reasoning, then, the defender of the bond and the promoter of justice cannot issue the summons.[17]

The summons is to be consigned to the defendant. If there are several defendants in the same lawsuit, several copies of the summons must be made, so that a single copy can be sent to each defendant.[18] If only one or several of many co-defendants are summoned, the judicial procedure is invalid relative to those who are not cited. If they later take part in the trial, they may but they are not obliged to acknowledge as valid the acts of procedure that have already been executed in the case. They can insist that those acts of procedure are null, and that the trial be renewed from the beginning. Of course the acts which have to do with the merits of the case retain their proper value.[19]

This was the interpretation given to this provision in the pre-Code law. Since the present legislation does not depart from the earlier law in this regard, but retains the sanction of nullity as to

---

tionem vel spontaneam comparitionem, qualis non est ea comparitio, quae per errorem putatur obligatoria." Cf. Roberti, *De Processibus,* I (1. ed.), n. 288, p. 436; Coronata, *Institutiones,* III, n. 1249, nota 2.

[15] Canons 1723; 1894, 1°.

[16] Canons 1712, § 1; 1715, § 1; Roberti, *De Processibus,* I (1. ed.), n. 288, p. 435.

[17] Cf. Vermeersch-Creusen, *Epitome,* III, n. 145.

[18] Canon 1712, § 2; Roberti, *De Processibus,* I (1. ed.), nn. 292, 293; Coronata, *Institutiones,* III, n. 1242; Wernz-Vidal, *Ius Canonicum,* VI, n. 386; Muñiz, *Procèdimientos Eclèsiasticos,* III, n. 157, p. 121, nota 3.

[19] Canons 1642, § 1; 1723.

the regulations governing the legitimate summons, this same interpretation still obtains.[20]

In order to be legitimate, the written summons must in its content first of all express the precept of the judge to the defendant to appear in court. This precept may for the sake of prudence and of urbanity be tempered to resemble a polite invitation; however, it must not entirely lose its perceptive nature.[21]

Secondly, the legitimate summons must designate the judge who issues the precept for appearance in court. The Code does not demand, but canonists recommend, that a delegated judge should intimate that his jurisdiction is delegated, since the precise reason for the judge's identifying himself is to allow the defendant to ascertain whether or not he is competent or suspect.[22] Some canonists even suggest that, unless the delegation is publicly known, a copy of it should be transmitted with the summons.[23] Since the Code does not require that any intimation of the delegated jurisdiction be given, omission of the mention of it does not render the summons illegitimate in the invalidating sense of canon 1894, 1°.[24]

If the tribunal is a collegiate one, it is fitting that the names of the individual judges be indicated in the summons, so that the defendant may immediately ascertain whether he considers any of them prejudiced concerning the case. However, the summons will not be invalid if it is issued only by the presiding recording judge or by the (*iudex instructor*). The practice of the Rota is to have

---

[20] Canons 1712, § 2; 1723; 1894, 1°. Cf. canon 6, 2°; Wernz-Vidal, *Ius Canonicum,* VI, n. 386; Hanssen, *op. cit.,* p. 96; De Luca, *Theatrum Veritatis et Iustitiae,* XV, disc. 9, nn. 35-38.

[21] Canon 1715, § 1; Roberti, *De Processibus,* I (1. ed.), n. 290; Wernz-Vidal, *Ius Canonicum,* VI, n. 386, nota 36. The regulations for certain matrimonial cases permit such a form of summons: "Citatio parti et testi fit per litteras in modum invitationis, tamen praeceptive."—S.C. de Sacramentis, *Regulae Servandae in Processibus super Matrimonio Rato et non Consummato,* 7 maii 1923, n. 36—*AAS,* XV (1923), 389 ss.

[22] Canon 1715, § 1; cf. canon 200, § 2; Wernz-Vidal, *op. cit.,* VI, n. 386; Roberti, *op. cit.,* I (1. ed.), n. 290.

[23] Wernz-Vidal, *loc. cit.;* Lega-Bartoccetti, *Commentarius,* II, 529; Coronata, *Institutiones,* III, n. 1242.

[24] Cf. canon 1715, § 1.

the summons issued in the name of the examining and recording auditor (*ponens*).[25]

Thirdly, the summons must indicate, at least in general terms, the nature of the cause for which the defendant is being summoned. The notice should normally contain a clear statement of the claim and the legal basis upon which it rests, so that the defendant can ascertain the nature of the suit and deliberate whether to yield or to contest the claim. Since the Code requires only a general indication of the cause, the summons will rarely be invalid on this account unless no mention whatever is made of it.[26]

Fourthly, the summons must rightly identify the plaintiff and the defendant. They are to be designated by their names and surnames.[27] The defendant, if his name remains unknown, can be designated by names of certain qualities or in connection with his office, as long as he is sufficiently determined for the precluding of any possible mistaken identity.[28]

When the defendant is a juridic person or a moral body, the proper appellation should be used. Moreover, when the defendant does not have the free administration of the goods that are in dispute, some physical person should also be specified who is to supply the procedural incapacity of the defendant. It is into this person's hands that the summons should be delivered. He is to be properly designated by name and surname, and the title in virtue of which he is convened should be additionally mentioned.[29]

The Sacred Roman Rota, in the appeal of the case of Froberger versus the Editors of *Petrusblätter* (at Trier), decided that the

---

[25] Coronata, *Institutiones,* III, n. 1242; Wernz-Vidal, *Ius Canonicum,* VI, n. 386, nota 35; Roberti, *De Processibus,* I, n. 290; S.C. de Sacramentis, instr., *Provida Mater,* 15 aug. 1936, Art. 76, § 2—*AAS,* XXVIII (1936), 330.

[26] Canon 1715, § 1; Wernz-Vidal, *op. cit.,* VI, n. 387; Roberti, *op. cit.,* I, n. 291.

[27] Canon 1715, § 1.

[28] ". . . contingere posse ut nomen eius iudici sit ignotum; tunc sufficiet hanc personam designare huiusmodi qualitate aut officio, quae non possunt convenire nisi illi soli, et ita personam citandam perfecte determinent."—S.R.R., *Treviren* (Diffamationis), 15 maii 1913, coram R.P.D. Seraphino Many—*AAS,* V (1913), 285.

[29] Roberti, *De Processibus,* I (1. ed.), n. 291; Wernz-Vidal, *Ius Canonicum,* VI, n. 386.

summons was null and void since it had not been directed to a specified person. The bishop's court had simply summoned the editors.[30] Hence, if a collegiate or a non-collegiate moral person is named defendant in a suit, the corresponding rector or administrator should be designated in the summons. If it is a case of minors or of those who lack the use of reason, the parents or the guardians should be cited; however, in spiritual matters children who enjoy the use of reason and who have completed their fourteenth year of age can be summoned directly. Unless the judge decrees otherwise, then in contentious cases, when the defendant is one whose prodigality has caused his reduction to the state of a ward, or when suit is entered against one who has less than ordinary stability of mind, the summons should be directed to the legally appointed curator or guardian.[31]

Fifthly, the summons must clearly indicate the place and the time in which the defendant is to appear in court for the joinder of issue.[32] The indicated place must be within the territory subject to the jurisdiction of the tribunal, for a judge cannot execute valid judicial acts outside his own territory except in the circumstances defined in canon 1637.[33]

The time scheduled for the defendant's appearance is to be stated according to the year, month, day and hour.[34] Bartoccetti thinks that an implied designation of the hour may suffice, i.e., if the hour is not specified, then those hours are understood which the ordinary

---

[30] *Treviren,* 15 maii 1913—*AAS,* V (1913), 284.

[31] Canon 1713; cf. canons 1648-1654; Roberti, *De Processibus,* I (1. ed.), n. 291; Coronata, *Institutiones,* III, n. 1241, p. 150.

[32] Canon 1715, § 1.

[33] Cf. *supra,* p. 97 ff. Unless the local ordinary has designated some other place within his territory, the designation of the ordinary seat of the diocesan tribunal is to be assumed. When its location is well known to the defendant, this implied designation may be sufficient; however, in most cases it will be necessary to mention the city, street, building, and even the room in which the defendant is to appear. The detailed address is of special importance when the case is to be tried by a delegated judge, since he does not have any permanent place wherein he holds court.—Cf. Coronata, *Institutiones,* III, n. 1242; Roberti, *De Processibus,* I (1. ed.), n. 290; Lega-Bartoccetti, *Commentarius,* II, 530.

[34] Canon 1715, § 1.

has fixed by public decree for regular access to the diocesan court. On the contrary, it appears that an express designation of the hour is required under sanction of invalidity to the same extent as with reference to the other requisites for a legitimate summons.[35]

While the law prohibits judicial procedure on holy days, it does not, as it did in the pre-Code legislation, invalidate judicial acts executed on these days.[36] Hence, if the summons explicitly prescribes that the defendant appear on a holy day, it is not invalid, and the defendant must comply. If no such explicit precept is manifested, the defendant can appear on the next following day which is not a holy day.[37]

The determination of the time within which the defendant must appear in court is discretionary with the judge. It should be of sufficient duration to allow for necessary preparation. If it is too brief, the summons is not invalid, but the defendant has just cause for not appearing, or, if he does appear, he may seek more time in which to deliberate. If such a brief period expires and the judge issues a decree of contempt of court, the defendant without any prejudice is to be admitted to the case if he appears in court within a reasonable time.[38]

The final requirement for the written summons is that the signatures of the judge or of his auditor and of the notary fortify it and that the seal of the tribunal be stamped upon it.[39]

Canon 1712 states that the summons is to be written on the bill of complaint or joined to it. However, the Code does not precisely demand that the introductory *libellus* should be transmitted to the defendant with the summons. Hence, if the requirements of canon 1715 have been fulfilled, any failure to include the bill of complaint does not render the summons illegitimate in the invalidating sense of canon 1723.[40] Ordinarily it will be advantageous to include the bill of complaint. Since all the elements which must be related in

---

[35] *Commentarius,* II, 530; cf. canon 1638.

[36] Canon 1639; c. 5, X, *de feriis,* II, 9.

[37] Canon 1635.

[38] Wernz-Vidal, *Ius Canonicum,* VI, n. 386; Hanssen, *De Sanctione Nullitatis in Processu Canonico,* p. 98.

[39] Canon 1715, § 2.

[40] Coronata, *Institutiones,* III, n. 1241.

the summons will be contained in a properly constructed bill of complaint, there is no reason why the judge cannot summon the defendant by sending him a copy of the introductory petition to which he has added his precept to appear.[41]

The judicial summons will be invalid, and thus will occasion invalidity for the subsequent acts of procedure in the trial, if it is not duly served.[42] The Code mentions three methods by which the summons may be legitimately served: by courier, by mail, and by edict. The regular canonical method is to consign the written summons to the defendant wherever he may be by courier or by any approved messenger.[43]

The present legislation settles the question that was disputed by pre-Code authors concerning the power of the courier to enter the territory of another jurisdiction to serve the summons.[44] The Code indicates that the service of the summons is not an act that postulates any power of jurisdiction, for it allows the summons to be consigned to the defendant wherever he may be. For this purpose the courier may enter another diocese if the judge deems it advisable and directs him to do so. The order of the judge to enter the other diocese is essential to the valid service of the summons in such a case.[45]

The primary direction of the law is that the written summons be handed to the defendant personally. However, if the defendant is not found at his dwelling, the summons can be left with some member of the family, or with a servant of the defendant, provided that

---

[41] Roberti, *De Processibus,* I (1. ed.), n. 291, p. 439; Wernz-Vidal, *Ius Canonicum,* VI, n. 387.

[42] Canon 1723.

[43] Canons 1712, § 2; 1717, § 1; 1721, § 1; 1719; 1720; 1591, § 1; 1592.

[44] Cf. Lega, *De Iudiciis Ecclesiasticis,* I, Vol. I, lib. I, n. 408; Schmalzgrueber, lib. II, tit. 4, n. 23; De Luca, *Theatrum Veritatis et Justitiae,* XV, pars I, disc. 9, n. 17.

[45] Canons 1717, §§ 1, 2; 1723. Lega-Bartoccetti (*Commentarius,* II, 531) and Noval (*De Iudiciis,* n. 400) stated that the courier may not enter another jurisdiction without an order from the judge to do so. Blat (*De Processibus,* n. 213) held that the order of the judge is merely a condition for the licitness of the act. Hanssen (*op. cit.,* p. 100) says that an implicit order of the judge seems to suffice for the valid service of the summons in another jurisdiction.

the person in question is willing to accept it, promises to give it to the defendant without delay, and is qualified to testify to his having received it.[46] Hence the summons is not validly served if it is deposited at a dwelling where no one is present, or if the person to whom it is entrusted does not promise to present it to the defendant, or if he refuses to accept it, or if he does not have sufficient intellectual powers to testify later on that he received the summons.[47]

When because of the distance or for some other reason[48] it is difficult to serve the summons, the judge can order it to be transmitted through the public mails, provided that the letter is registered and a return receipt is demanded. For the same reasons the judge may send the summons in any other manner which according to the law and the condition of the respective country is considered safest.[49] The Code allows a certain liberty in regard to this substitute method of transmitting the summons. It gives to the judge an option of using the public mails or of having recourse to some

---

[46] Canons 1717, §§ 1, 3; 1757, § 1; Roberti, *De Processibus,* I (1. ed.), n. 294, p. 443.

[47] Lega-Bartoccetti (*Commentarius,* II, 532, 533) state that canon 1717, § 3, contains only a demonstrative list of the possible courses which the messenger can pursue when he is unable to locate the defendant personally. Consequently they say that the summons can be left with responsible neighbors or affixed to the home of the defendant. This opinion cannot be accepted in view of the fact that the canon allows the courier no discretionary powers, but clearly states that, when he cannot consign the summons to the defendant or to a member of his family or to a servant of his household, he must return it to the judge. Other canonists uniformly agree to this interpretation. Cf. Coronata, *Institutiones,* III, n. 1245; Roberti, *De Processibus,* I (1. ed.), n. 294, p. 443; Wernz-Vidal, *Ius Canonicum,* VI, n. 389, p. 335; Blat, *De Processibus,* n. 213, p. 241; Prümmer, *Manuale Iuris Canonici* (6. ed., Friburgi Brisgoviae: Herder, 1933), p. 582. Augustine, *Commentary,* VII, 169; Woywod, *A Practical Commentary on the Code of Canon Law,* II, n. 1677; Doheny, *Canonical Procedure,* I, 164. It may also be pointed out that in the preliminary drafts of the Code the suggestion of leaving the summons with neighbors was considered, but not accepted.—Roberti, *Schemata,* F, Can. 185, § 4, nota 13.

[48] E.g., inclement weather, poor roads, danger inherent in the journey—cf. Lega-Bartoccetti, *Commentarius,* II, 533.

[49] Canon 1719.

other safe means of conveyance according to the conditions of the locality.[50]

This second method of serving the summons is to be used only where there is difficulty in delivering the summons by courier, and only in pursuance of an order of the judge. Since under any consideration the Code allows the use of this method when a personal serving of the summons proves difficult, recourse to this method will hardly ever be invalid in consequence of the lack of a sufficient reason; however, before it can be validly adopted, an order of the judge is required. An implicit order of the judge may suffice, e.g., one that is implied in the customary practice of the tribunal. An implicit order would at least save the summons from invalidity, for the provision of canon 1719, *"iussu Iudicis,"* would have been sufficiently complied with for a legitimate serving of the summons.[51]

A third method of serving the summons is allowed when after diligent inquiry the whereabouts of the defendant remains unknown. This is the summons by edict. The edictal summons is posted on the doors of the curia for a period of time to be determined by the judge, and it is also to be inserted in a public journal. If not both of these means can be used, then either one will suffice.[52]

Lega-Bartoccetti advance as a valid reason for employing but one of these two ways of publishing the edictal summons the fact that the other one will be most certainly inefficacious.[53] Neither the Code nor any of the commentators mentions how often the edict should be inserted in the newspaper when that means is adopted for the publication of the edict. Hence it can be argued that even if it were published only once, the subsequent acts of procedure in the

---

[50] Other means of transmitting the summons may be available through the ministry of the curia in the diocese where the defendant dwells, or of his pastor, or of the courier of a lay tribunal. Cf. Coronata, *Institutiones,* III, n. 1246; Roberti, *De Processibus,* I (1. ed.), n. 294, p. 444; Wernz-Vidal, *Ius Canonicum,* VI, n. 389, p. 535.

[51] Canons 1719; 1723. Cf. Beste, *Introductio in Codicem,* p. 812; Regatillo *Institutiones Iuris Canonici,* II, n. 528.

[52] Canon 1720, §§ 1, 2.

[53] *Commentarius,* II, 535.

case would not be invalid on the grounds of an illegitimate summons. Commentators do mention that the official diocesan newspaper is preferably the one to be chosen for the publication of the edictal summons. The choice of the paper, however, should be controlled by the consideration of the best means of intimating the summons to the defendant.[54]

By its very nature the edictal method of publishing the summons is imperfect; however, it suffices when the whereabouts of the defendant cannot be determined, and the process will not be invalid, unless no previous investigation was made for the purpose of locating the defendant.[55]

The regulations for the legitimate serving of the summons according to one of the three methods prescribed by the Code carry with them the sanction of nullity with reference to the very summons, to the subsequent acts of the procedure, and to the definitive sentence;[56] but the provisions of law governing the conduct of the messenger after he has consigned the written summons to the defendant, i.e., the fact that he must sign the document, marking the date and the hour at which he handed it to the defendant, etc.,[57] are not binding under this sanction since they do not come within the scope of the provision, *"scheda . . . legitime intimata,"* for the reason simply that all of these acts occur subsequent to the legitimately served summons. The contrary opinion, namely that these regulations bind under pain of invalidity, as held by Coronata,[58] is not warranted either by the text or by the context of canons 1721 and 1723.[59]

It does not appear either that the written report which the messenger must render to the judge concerning his work in serving the summons is essential for the validity of the summons; however, if the messenger fails to make his report, it may be difficult to establish the lawfulness of the summons if it is ever questioned.[60]

---

[54] Lega-Bartoccetti, *loc. cit.;* Wernz-Vidal, *op. cit.,* VI, n. 389, p. 335; Roberti, *De Processibus,* I (1. ed.), n. 294, p. 445.

[55] Canons 1720, § 1; 1723.

[56] Canons 1723; 1894, 1°.

[57] Canon 1721.

[58] *Institutiones,* III, n. 1248.

[59] Cf. canon 18.

[60] Cf. canon 1722.

The regulations governing the content and the serving of the summons must be meticulously observed; otherwise the summons is illegitimate with the consequence that the subsequent acts of procedure in the trial and the definitive sentence are null and void.[61] Unless the unlawfulness of the summons is beyond all doubt, it should not be so considered without a previous investigation and declaration of its nature by the judge.[62]

The fact that the defendant does not learn of the summons does not render it illegitimate. As long as there are observed the formalities of law which normally suffice for informing the defendant that he is being sued, the summons is legitimate and sufficient for the constitution of a valid trial.[63] However, if it happens that the defendant fails to comply with the summons, and that he does not offer an explanation for not appearing or at least not a valid one, the judge cannot proceed to pronounce him guilty of contempt of court, unless it is sufficiently evident that the summons was legitimately issued and brought to the notice of the defendant within due time, or at least should have come to his notice.[64]

The foregoing rules govern the initial summons of the defendant, and they are to be followed also whenever a summons is needed for other judicial acts. For subsequent summonses, however, as long as these regulations are observed substantially the acts of the process and of the ensuing sentence will not be invalid on their account, since the Code permits that such summonses be adapted to the diverse nature of the various acts for which a summons is required.[65]

The plaintiff also is to be notified by the court to appear before the judge for the joinder of issue on a specified day and at a fixed hour. An informal notice suffices, since the law does not provide

[61] Canons 1723; 1894, 1°; Roberti, *De Processibus,* I (1. ed.), n. 288, p. 436; Wernz-Vidal, *Ius Canonicum,* VI, n. 386; Coronata, *Institutiones,* III, n. 1242. The clear statement of canon 1723 leaves no room for the interpretation of Lega-Bartoccetti (*Commentarius,* II, 539) that, if the regulations governing the citation are observed *quoad substantiam,* the sanction of nullity attached to them cannot be invoked.

[62] Cf. Lega-Bartoccetti, *op. cit.,* II, 539.

[63] Cf. Roberti, *De Processibus,* I (1. ed.), n. 294, p. 445.

[64] Canon 1843, § 1, 1°, 2°.

[65] Canon 1724.

any predetermined form for the summons of the plaintiff.[66] Moreover, no sanction of nullity is attached to the regulation governing the notification of the plaintiff; however, when the plaintiff fails to appear, then the judge, before he can declare him guilty of contempt of court must issue a second notification, and this time it should be a formal summons.[67]

At this point in the consideration of judicial nullity, notice should be taken of one of the courses permitted to the defendant after the judge has declared the plaintiff contumacious.[68] He is allowed to petition the court for a declaration of nullity of all the acts that have up to that time been executed in the case.[69] This right is especially efficacious when the trial has already begun and the plaintiff has failed to continue the prosecution of it. In virtue of this right all the acts of the case, not only the acts of procedure but also the acts which regard the merits of the case, can be declared null and void. Consequently, they will have no legal value whatsoever if the case is ever again introduced in court.[70]

ARTICLE 3. THE JOINDER OF ISSUE

The joinder of issue, in which the object or matter of the trial is definitely established, consists in the formal denial of the plaintiff's claim by the defendant, made with the intention of contesting the case judicially.[71] Ordinarily for the joinder of issue the Code requires no other formality than that the claim of the plaintiff and the denial of the defendant be inserted in the record.[72]

The joinder of issue, embodying as it does the specific grounds upon which the contention is based and disputed, constitutes the

---

[66] Canon 1712, § 3.

[67] Canon 1849; 1724; Roberti, *De Processibus,* II, n. 410.

[68] The other courses allowed him are that he petition the court either that he may be discharged in the case, or that he may be definitively freed from the claim or charge of the plaintiff, or that the trial may, even in the absence of the plaintiff, be conducted to the end.—Canon 1850, § 3.

[69] Canon 1850, § 3.

[70] ". . . ut . . . nulla habeantur omnia eo usque gesta."—Canon 1850, § 3; Roberti, *De Processibus,* II, n. 411, p. 138.

[71] Canon 1726.

[72] Canon 1727.

fundamental basis and the cornerstone of the whole canonical trial. Consequently one may well ask if its omission constitutes an essential deficiency in the judicial process, so that the process itself would be rendered completely invalid.[73] However, no formal joinder of issue is required for the validity of the trial. As long as the object of the controversy is determined, the judicial process will not be lacking any essential constitutive element, and nowhere in the present legislation is the joinder of issue required under positive sanction of nullity. The claim of the plaintiff will be known both from the bill of complaint and from the judicial summons.[74] Any denial of this claim by the defendant, made with the intention of contesting it judicially, will serve to determine the object of the legal dispute. The Sacred Roman Rota has sustained the validity of trials in which the joinder of issue was omitted, inasmuch as despite the omission the litigants were fully aware of the object of the trial.[75]

That a formal joinder of issue is not absolutely necessary for the validity of the trial appears also from the procedure that is permitted when the defendant is contumacious. In such an instance the trial can be conducted and the definitive sentence pronounced even though there has not been any joinder of issue.[76]

There is greater necessity for the formal joinder of issue when the case is difficult and involved, viz., when the petition of the plaintiff is neither clear nor simple and the denial of the defendant is beset with difficulties. In such a case if the formal joinder of issue is neglected, it may happen that the object of the dispute will remain undetermined, so that the trial will be lacking an essential constitutive element.[77]

---

[73] Cf. Noval, *De Iudiciis,* n. 411, p. 291.

[74] Canons 1708; 1715, § 1.

[75] S.R.R. *Luganen.* (Iurium), 5 mart. 1915, coram R.P.D. Guillelmo Sebastianelli—*AAS,* VII (1915), 240; S.R.R., *Querelae Nullitatis et Nullitatis Matrimonii,* 8 febr. 1936, coram R.P.D. Andrea Jullien, dec. XII, n. 6. ". . . De litis autem contestatione in specie, haec adnotentur: attentis supra dictis perpensisque can. 1726-1728, patet quod formalis contestatio litis nec lege naturali nec lege positiva hodierna ad validitatem iudicii requiritur. Requiruntur vero actoris petito reique contradictio, ut de obiecto iudicii determinato fiat disceptatio utque iudex de eo pronuntiare possit."—*Decisiones,* XXVIII (1936), 120.

[76] Canon 1844, § 2.

[77] Canon 1728; cf. Wernz-Vidal, *Ius Canonicum,* VI, nn. 399, 400.

ARTICLE 4. NULLITY IN THE DEVELOPMENT OF THE TRIAL

In accord with the tenor of the present legislation to restrict the number of judicial nullities, the positive law of the Code attaches to only a few of the regulations governing the actual development of the trial the sanction of judicial nullity, and by the natural law only the absence of proof for the cause and the failure to allow the defendant an opportunity to present a legitimate defense can be considered as essential deficiencies in the judicial process.[78]

A. *Regulations for a Valid Judicial Renouncement*

The positive law of the Code contains certain regulations for the valid renouncement of a judicial hearing and for the valid renouncement of any or all of the acts of the process. These regulations appear to be for the protection of the other litigant when the one party takes advantage of his right to renounce the hearing or the acts of the process. The Code grants to the plaintiff the right to renounce the hearing at any stage and in any degree of the trial, and it permits both the plaintiff and the defendant to renounce all or some of the acts of the process.[79]

In order that any judicial renouncement be valid, certain conditions must be fulfilled. The renouncement is to be made in writing and signed by the party or by his procurator on having a specific mandate.[80] The reason for this provision of the law is quite evident, since the act of renouncement pertains to the merits of the case, and the notice of it should be in the record for future reference if the same case is again introduced into court. When there is question of the renouncement of a certain act or acts, it must also

[78] Cf. canon 1680, § 1; S.R.R., *Querelae Nullitatis et Nullitatis Matrimonii,* 8 febr. 1936, coram R.P.D. Andrea Jullien, dec. XII, n. 6: "De ordine iudiciali [attendantur] quae iudicium constituunt essentialiter, tam igitur in iure veteri quam in iure Codicis. . . . 'Iuris naturalis sunt petitio actoris, citatio rei, probatio causae, eiusdemque defensio, decisio illius, et sententiae pronuntiatio; nam haec ad substantiam iudicii pertinent, et talia sunt ut sine illis causa controversa recte et rite discuti atque decidi nequeat.' "—*Decisiones,* XXVIII (1936), 119.

[79] Canon 1740, § 1.

[80] Canon 1740, § 2.

be in writing, so that its bearing on the particular case will be evident from the record.[81]

Judicial renouncement is one of the functions for which a procurator needs a specific mandate. His ordinary powers of attorney do not enable him to renounce the hearing or any of the acts of the case.[82] The judicial renouncement must be made known to the other party and be accepted by him or at least not called in question by him. The judge must allow this party a reasonable amount of time for considering whether he wishes to oppose the renouncement. When this period has elapsed without any remonstrance from the party, he is presumed to have accepted it.[83] Authors agree that the acceptance can be limited and conditioned; hence the defendant can indicate that he accepts the renouncement provided that he will not be molested a second time in this same matter by this same plaintiff.[84]

The final condition for a valid renouncement is that it be admitted by the judge. The Code does not demand that to this end the judge issue a decree, but authors recommend that he do so for the sake of the record.[85] The judge should not admit the renouncement when to do so would prove prejudicial to a third party or to the

---

[81] Cf. Lega-Bartoccetti, *Commentarius,* II, 598.

[82] Canon 1740, § 2. Authors raise the question of the power of the representatives of moral persons or of physical persons who lack the free administration of their affairs to renounce the hearing in a trial. Lega-Bartoccetti (*Commentarius,* II, 600) and Roberti, *De Processibus,* II, n. 316, p. 14) state that they need a special commission, since the act of renouncing the hearing exceeds the ordinary powers of administration. Coronata (*Institutiones,* III, n. 1266) says that a special mandate is not required, at least not for the renouncement of the trial in its first hearing. While such representatives should, before they renounce the hearing or any of the acts of the process, seek the consent or the advice of those for whom they appear, yet in the absence of any express or equivalent invalidating clause in the law, it cannot be said that the renouncement carried out by such representatives apart from a specific mandate is invalid.

[83] Canon 1740, § 2; Wernz-Vidal, *Ius Canonicum,* VI, n. 415.

[84] Roberti, *De Processibus,* II, n. 316, p. 14; Coronata, *Institutiones,* III, n. 1265. Woywod, *A Practical Commentary on the Code of Canon Law,* II, n. 1695.

[85] Roberti, *op. cit.,* II, 15; Coronata, *Institutiones,* III, n. 1267; Wernz-Vidal, *loc. cit.*

common good, or when the renouncement is opposed by the other litigant, or by the promoter of justice, or by the defender of the bond. When there is opposition to the renouncement the matter should be treated as an incidental question.[86] The judge should admit the renouncement in cases of private interest when the prescribed conditions for its validity are verified.[87] If in cases of public concern the plaintiff wishes to renounce the hearing, and the judge permits him to do so, then the promoter of justice or the defender of the bond may continue the case in his stead.[88]

Judicial acts that are validly renounced lose their juridic value, and they cannot be considered by the judge in his determining of the sentence.[89]

B. *Prejudicial Attempts against the Rights of Litigants*

By the positive law of the Code prejudicial attempts against the rights of a party or parties in a trial are *ipso iure* invalid.[90] The present legislature thereby settles the pre-Code controversy over this question. Some authors had held that the acts connected with a prejudicial attempt were not invalid but rescissible.[91]

A prejudicial attempt is any innovation which is detrimental to a litigant, and to which he does not consent regarding the matter in judicial dispute or regarding the terms or periods of time assigned by law or by the judge for the performance of certain judicial acts. The author of the innovation may be one of the parties against the other, or the judge against one of the parties or against both of them.[92] The object of the innovation may be either the subject matter of the trial or the terms assigned for the

[86] Wernz-Vidal, *loc. cit.*

[87] Coronata, *Institutiones,* III, n. 1266; Roberti, *De Processibus,* II, n. 316, p. 15.

[88] Wernz-Vidal, *Ius Canonicum,* VI, n. 415.

[89] Canon 1741; Wernz-Vidal, *loc. cit.*

[90] Canon 1855, § 1.

[91] Cf. Reiffenstuel, lib. II, tit. 16, n. 21-22; Lega, *De Iudiciis,* Vol. I, lib. I, n. 583.

[92] Canon 1854; Coronata, *Institutiones,* III, n. 1385; Roberti, *De Processibus,* II, n. 430; Wernz-Vidal, *Ius Canonicum,* VI, n. 570; Lega-Bartoccetti, *Commentarius,* II, 894; Augustine, *Commentary,* VII, 298.

executing of certain judicial acts. Attempts to change or make changes in the subject matter of the trial ordinarily are extrajudicial acts. For instance, the alienation of property when the title to it is legally disputed is not directly related to any procedural act in the case. While such attempts are automatically void, they do not render the judicial process invalid, since they have no causal connection with any procedural act; consequently they do not fall within the scope of this dissertation.[93]

Attempts, however, to change or make changes in the terms or periods of time are procedural acts. If such acts are prejudicial to the rights of the other party, they are not only invalid in themselves, but they may render invalid other acts which depend on them.[94] Thus a peremptory time is to be fixed by the judge for submitting to the court the names and domiciles of witnesses and the articles concerning which they are to be questioned. Thus the judge may be guilty of a prejudicial attempt if he grants a new term for this purpose without the consent of the other litigant.[95]

The Rota declared a definitive sentence invalid for the reason that it constituted a prejudicial attempt against a litigant, for it was pronounced while in the same case an appeal was pending from an interlocutory sentence which had a definitive effect.[96]

Roberti states[97] that generally any inversion of the judicial order which is detrimental to a litigant can constitute a prejudicial attempt. This statement is misleading, for not every act of disobedience on the part of the litigant, nor every act of negligence on the part of the judge, is to be considered as a prejudicial attempt and consequently as automatically invalid.[98]

In view of the tenor of the present legislation in regard to the nullity of acts,[99] all the conditions specified in canon 1854 for a

---

[93] Cf. Wernz-Vidal, *Ius Canonicum,* VI, n. 572; Roberti, *De Processibus,* II, n. 431.

[94] Canons 1855, § 1; 1680, § 2.

[95] Canons 1761; 1854.

[96] S.R.R., *Rheginen.* (Nullitatis Matrimonii Incidentis), 28 iul. 1938, coram R.P.D. Guillelmo Heard, dec. LI—*Decisiones,* XXX (1938), 472-477; cf. canon 1880, 6°.

[97] *De Processibus,* II, n. 432, p. 154.

[98] Cf. Wernz-Vidal, *Ius Canonicum,* VI, n. 574.

[99] Canon 1680.

prejudicial attempt will have to be verified before the act can be considered *ipso iure* invalid. These conditions are: a.) that the prejudicial attempt be an innovation in reference to the subject matter of the trial, or in reference to the terms fixed by law or by the judge for the executing of certain judicial acts; b.) that the innovation take place while the case is pending, viz., during that period which runs from the moment that the initial citation was legitimately served until the end of the trial, whether it be terminated by means of a definitive sentence or in any other way;[100] c.) that it be attempted either by one party against the other, or by the judge against one or both of the parties; hence an innovation by a third person would not constitute a prejudicial attempt; d.) that it be detrimental to the party or parties; in this respect it is to be noted that even an act performed in good faith may be prejudicial;[101] and e.) that it be executed against the will of the other party.[102]

This last condition is of special significance, for though prejudicial attempts are *ipso iure* invalid, the nullity of the act will not arise unless the injured party opposes it, for the Code expressly postulates this dissent of the opponent as a necessary condition for a prejudicial attempt. However, this dissent is presumed in cases wherein the injured party does not realize the detrimental nature of the act, or does not know that the prejudicial act has been executed. The judge does not *ex officio* have to reveal the prejudicial attempt to the party unless it is detrimental to the public good, or to the poor, or to minors, or to others who enjoy the protection which the law gives to minors.[103]

Roberti remarks that in view of the augmented powers which the judge enjoys under the present legislation, and in view also of the public nature of the canonical precedure, a prejudicial attempt against the rights of a litigant will rarely occur.[104]

---

[100] Cf. Roberti, *De Processibus,* II, n. 430, p. 153.

[101] Cf. Roberti, *op. cit.,* II, n. 432, p. 155.

[102] Canon 1854; Coronata, *Institutiones,* III, n. 1385; Augustine, *Commentary,* VII, 298, 299.

[103] Canon 1854: ". . . parte dissentiente"; canon 1682; Coronata, *op. cit.,* III, n. 1386; Muñiz, *Procedimientos Eclésiasticos,* III, n. 235, p. 183, in nota.

[104] Roberti, *De Processibus,* II, n. 430, p. 152.

C. *The Introduction of New Proof after the Closing of the Case*

Of a similar nature to the question of the prejudicial attempt is that of the introduction of new proofs after the closing of the case; however, the regulations regarding this matter carry with them their own invalidating clause. There is an explicit nullifying clause attached to the provision which forbids the judge to deny the right of a legitimate defense against proofs that have been introduced after the closing of the case. When the judge believes that new proofs should be admitted, he must give a hearing to the opponent and allow him sufficient time to acquaint himself with and defend himself against the new proofs; otherwise the trial is invalid.[105]

---

[105] Canon 1861, § 2.

CHAPTER VII

Nullity in the Definitive Sentence

ARTICLE 1. DEFICIENCES IN THE DEFINITIVE SENTENCE

The sentence which terminates the formal judicial process is null when it is vitiated with some substantial defect which is extrinsic to the sentence.[1] This defect originates in the sentence when the very written act which is the sentence labors under some substantial deficiency. It is derived from the judicial process when the sentence, which of itself is perfect, is the result of an invalid process, or when it is based on invalid acts of the process.[2]

The nullity of a judicial sentence can be irremediable or remediable. As is to be expected, an irremediable nullity is one that results from a serious defect, while a remediable nullity is occasioned by a comparatively minor deficiency. Roberti[3] says that the distinction between the two classes lies in the diverse periods of time during which an action for the declaration of the respective nullities is obtainable at law. The right to an action for a declaration of nullity of a remediable null sentence lapses through legal prescription after three months from the day of the publication of the sentence, while the right to have a sentence declared irremediably null expires only after thirty years from the day the sentence was published. Moreover, an irremediable nullity may be opposed by means of a judicial exception at any future time.[4]

---

[1] Canons 1892; 1894. An intrinsic substantial defect, e.g., an incorrect interpretation of the evidence upon which the sentence is based, should of itself render a sentence invalid, but usually such a defect is not readily apparent, and the sentence is rather considered unjust, so that the ordinary remedy against it is that of appeal. Cf. Wernz-Vidal, *Ius Canonicum*, VI, n. 614; Coronata, *Institutiones*, III, n. 1417.

[2] Roberti, *De Processibus*, II, n. 487.

[3] *Op. cit.*, n. 488.

[4] Canons 1893; 1895.

Other authors[5] state that the difference is based on the fact that the parties can yield their right to have a sentence declared null in consequence of a remediable nullity, while, because of the public good, their consent simply cannot sanate an irremediable nullity. Both opinions are correct; however, the latter one states more incisively the essential difference between the two classses of nullity, and it is more in harmony with the literal meaning of the terms remediable and irremediable.

The irremediable nullity of a sentence does not originate with the sentence. Rather, it derives from certain deficiencies in the prerequisites for the trial. It arises because the sentence has been issued by a judge who is absolutely incompetent, or in a collegiate tribunal by an insufficient number of judges in violation of canon 1576, § 1;[6] because at least one of the parties lacks the right to stand in judgment, and because of the absence of a legitimate mandate on the part of a procurator who attempted to represent a litigant in court.[7] These deficiencies and the ensuing irremediable nullity of the sentence to which they give rise have already been considered in this dissertation.[8] The discussion which follows will be concerned solely with the remediable nullities that can attach to the definitive sentence.

A sentence is vitiated with a remediable nullity: a.) when the legally called for summons was omitted; b.) when the motives for the decision are not included in the sentence (the sentences of the Apostolic Signatura, however, are valid even when the motives are omitted); c.) when the required signatures are lacking, i.e., the signatures of each judge and of the notary; and d.) when all or even any of the indications of the day, month, year, or place in which the sentence was given are missing.[9]

---

[5] Wernz-Vidal, *loc. cit.;* Vermeersch-Creusen, *Epitome,* III, n. 241, p. 102; Lega-Bartoccetti, *Commentarius,* II, 1016.

[6] When the judge is absolutely incompetent, all the acts of the case are null; when the number of judges is insufficient, only those acts are invalid which require the intervention of the entire collegiate tribunal. Coronata, *Institutiones,* III, n. 1418; Muñiz, *Procedimientos Eclesiásticos,* III, 502.

[7] Canon 1892.

[8] Cf. *supra,* pp. 73 ff.; 89 ff.; 105 ff.; 136 ff.

[9] Canon 1894; Roberti, *De Processibus,* II, n. 487; Wernz-Vidal, *Ius Canonicum,* VI, n. 622, p. 572.

The first cause of remediable nullity listed by canon 1894, namely the omission of the legally called for summons, has caused some difficulty, since the canon does not specify which summons it means. Lemieux[10] suggests that possibly this summons is not the initial summons, but the summons that is to be issued in connection with the publication of the sentence. However, the most that can be said of the omission of the summons for the publication of the sentence is that the sentence cannot be effective until it is properly published, not that it is invalid.[11]

Canon 1894, 1°, most certainly refers to the initial summons, for the Sacred Roman Rota has declared sentences invalid precisely because of the failure of the judge to summon the defendant for the joinder of issue or for any of the hearings of the trial.[12] A recently published decision stated that the Code in canon 1894, 1°, refers to the first summons by which the cause is introduced.[13] Authors generally agree that the summons referred to in canon 1894, 1°, is the one that is called for at the beginning of the trial.[14] This summons has already been treated at length in this treatise.[15]

The second cause for the remediable nullity of a sentence is

---

[10] *The Sentence in Ecclesiastical Procedure,* The Catholic University of America Canon Law Studies, n. 87 (Washington, D. C.: The Catholic University of America, 1934), p. 98.

[11] Wernz-Vidal, *Ius Canonicum,* VI, n. 622.

[12] S.R.R., *Querelae Nullitatis et Nullitatis Matrimonii,* 10 aug. 1929, coram R.P.D. Ubaldo Mannucci, dec. LI, n. 2—*Decisiones,* XXI (1929), 426; *Matiiten.* (Nullitatis Actorum et Sententiae), 3 iul. 1933; coram R.P.D. Francisco Parrillo, dec. XLVIII, n. 2—*Decisiones,* XXV (1933), 421; *Querelae Nullitatis et Nullitatis Matrimonii,* 8 febr. 1936, coram R.P.D. Andrea Jullien, dec. XII—*Decisiones,* XXVIII (1936), 119; *Tergestina* (Querelae Nullitatis et Nullitatis Matrimonii), 22 oct. 1936, coram R.P.D. Arcturo Wynen, dec. LXV, n. 2—*Decisiones,* XXVIII (1936), 621; *Viennen.* (Querelae Nullitatis et Nullitatis Matrimonii), 22 maii 1937, coram R.P.D. Alberto Canestri, dec. XXXV, n. 2—*Decisiones,* XXIX (1937), 354.

[13] S.R.R., *Querelae Nullitatis et Nullitatis Matrimonii,* 4 febr. 1939, coram R.P.D. Alberto Canestri, dec. X, n. 2—*Decisiones,* XXXI (1939), 85.

[14] Roberti, *De Processibus,* II, n. 489; Wernz-Vidal, *Ius Canonicum,* VI, n. 622; Lega-Bartoccetti, *Commentarius,* II, 1042; Coronata, *Institutiones,* III, n. 1418; Muñiz, *Procedimientos Eclesiásticos,* III, n. 503, nota 1.

[15] *Supra,* pp. 152 ff.

the omission of the motives or of the reasons for the decision. Hence, if either the reasons in fact or in law are omitted, the sentence is remediably null. Both must be given if the sentence is to stand. However, the law does not specify the number or the manner of formulation of these motives and reasons; hence, only the absolute failure to indicate either the reasons in fact or the reasons in law for the sentence would give rise to this form of invalidity. If false or irrelevant motives or reasons are alleged, there may be grounds for the plaint of nullity, and certainly there are grounds for appeal.[16]

The third cause of a remediable nullity in the definitive sentence is the omission of the signatures prescribed by law. The sentence must be signed by all the judges who participate in the decision and by the notary. Hence a sentence given by a collegiate tribunal and signed only by the presiding judge and the notary is invalid.[17] Doheny states that it is not necessary that the judge affix their signatures in the presence of one another. He also points out that when one or more of the judges of the collegiate tribunal who gave the decision inadvertently forgets to sign the sentence, this oversight can be corrected and the sentence rectified simply by a supplying of the missing signatures. The signatures can be supplied at any time within three months from the publication of the sentence, as long as the plaint of nullity has not been raised. After three months the litigants lose their right to challenge the validity of the sentence, and the sentence then stands.[18]

The last reason listed in the enumeration of the causes of remediable nullity in the sentence is the failure to indicate the complete date and the precise locality in which the sentence was issued. The year, month, day, and the place must be specified

---

[16] Canon 1894, 2°; Doheny, *Canonical Procedure,* I, 517; Roberti, *De Processibus,* II, n. 389, p. 224; Wernz-Vidal, *Ius Canonicum,* VI, n. 622, p. 571.

[17] Canons 1894, 3°; 1874, § 5; *PCI,* 14 iul. 1922: "Utrum ad norman can. 1874, § 5, et can. 1894, n. 3, nullitatis vitio laboret sententia lata a tribunali collegiali et subscripta tantum a praeside tribunalis et notario. Resp. Affirmative."—*AAS,* XIV (1922), 529.

[18] Doheny, *op. cit.,* I, 517. Cf. canons 1897, § 2; 1895; 1634, § 1.

with exactitude. If any one item is missing or is wrong, the sentence is null.[19]

A sentence that is vitiated with a remediable nullity can be sanated *"ab homine vel ab ipso iure."* It is said to be remedied *ab homine* when a party renounces his right to have the sentence declared null, or when the deficiency in the sentence is supplied for before the nullity is opposed. A remediably invalid sentence is sanated *ab ipso iure* when within three months from the day of the publication of the sentence the plaint of nullity is not proposed before the judge who pronounced the sentence.[20]

ARTICLE 2. THE INTERPRETATION OF CANONS 1892 AND 1894

There have been two schools of thought on the question whether or not the enumeration of the causes of invalid sentences in canons 1892 and 1894 is so complete that a sentence is not nullified in consequence of any procedural deficiency other than those which are therein listed. There are violations of procedural law which nullify certain acts of the trial, but the present legislation nowhere declares the invalidity of the sentence which concludes a trial wherein these violations occur. Thus the introduction of new proofs after the closing of the case without the granting to the other party of an opportunity of a legitimate defense with respect to them renders the trial invalid.[21]

Other examples of this type of procedural invalidity are the following: The renouncement of a judicial hearing or of any of the acts of the case is invalid if it is not carried out in the manner prescribed by law.[22] Judicial acts that are not written or at least signed by the notary are null and void.[23] In cases which require the presence of the promoter of justice or of the defender of the

---

[19] Canon 1894, 4°; Doheny, *op. cit.*, I, 518; Roberti, *De Processibus*, II, n. 489, p. 225; Wernz-Vidal, *Ius Canonicum*, VI, n. 622, p. 572.

[20] S.R.R., *Tergestina* (Querelae Nullitatis et Nullitatis Matrimonii), 22 oct. 1936, coram R.P.D. Arcturo Wynen, dec. LXV, n. 2—*Decisiones*, XXVIII (1936), 621.

[21] Canon 1861, § 2.

[22] Canon 1740, § 2.

[23] Canon 1585, § 1.

bond, the acts are invalid if these officials were not summoned, unless they were present without being summoned.[24] Acts which constitute a prejudicial attempt against the rights of the litigant are automatically null and void.[25]

It has been acridly disputed whether or not any of the above mentioned invalid acts will also invalidate the definitive sentence. Since the latest articles and works of the authors[26] who have considered this problem at length have appeared, the jurisprudence of the Sacred Roman Rota has become evident in this matter.[27] The clear and repeated decisions of the Sacred Rota can be said to have established a precedent which resolves the doubt of law which existed concerning the interpretation of canons 1892 and 1894. The Rota has espoused the strict interpretation, which states that these canons contain an all-inclusive list of the deficiencies which invalidate the definitive sentence.

This controversy over the interpretation of the canons on the remedy of the plaint of nullity is intimately connected with that concerning the interpretation of the phrase, "*praescriptum legis evidenter neglectum,*" in canon 1905 § 2, 4°—viz., whether the *restitutio in integrum* can be used against a sentence which is vitiated because of a neglect of a provision of procedural law.[28] The interpretation given to the canon on the plaint of nullity is

---

[24] Canon 1587, § 1.

[25] Canons 1854; 1855.

[26] Cf. Hanssen, *De Sanctione Nullitatis in Processu Canonico,* pp. 155-166; Regatillo, *Institutiones Iuris Canonici,* II, n. 687.

[27] S.R.R., *S. Iacobi de Chile* (Restitutionis in Integrum et Compromissi), 5 iul. 1927, coram R.P.D. Francisco Parrillo, dec. XXIV, nn. 4-11—*Decisiones,* XIX (1927), 276 sqq; *Matriten* (Nullitatis Actorum et Sententiae), 3 iul. 1933, coram R.P.D. Francisco Parrillo, dec. XLVIII, n. 2—*Decisiones,* XXV (1933), 420-423; *Parisien* (Nullitatis Matrimonii), 7 iul. 1934, coram R.P.D. Henrico Quattrocalo, dec. XL, nn. 6, 7—*Decisiones,* XXVI (1934), 349-350; *Querelae Nullitatis et Nullitatis Matrimonii,* 8 febr. 1936, coram R.P.D. Andrea Jullien, dec. XII, n. 6—*Decisiones,* XXVIII (1936), 119; *Tergestina* (Querelae Nullitatis et Nullitatis Matrimonii), 22 oct. 1936, coram R.P.D. Arcturo Wynen, dec. LXV, n. 2—*Ibid.,* p. 621 sqq.

[28] Cf. Feeney, *Restitutio in Integrum,* The Catholic University of America Canon Law Studies, n. 129 (Washington, D. C.: The Catholic University of America Press, 1941), pp. 111-130.

not necessarily dependent on the interpretation given to the phrase "*praescriptum legis evidenter neglectum*" of canon 1905, § 2, 4°.[29] For the sake of clarity and brevity, then, the writer will abstract from the controversy concerning the *restitutio* as much as possible in the discussion which follows:

Since the controversy on this question has been a major one, the opinions and the arguments for both sides will be set forth in the following pages. The decisions of the Roman Rota, which, in the opinion of the writer, definitely decide the question, will be set down in the conclusion of the article. The side of the controversy which supports the liberal and broad interpretation of the canons will be referred to as the opinion of Roberti, and the arguments for the strict interpretation will be mentioned as those of D'Angelo. Due credit, whenever necessary, will be given to the contributions of others to each opinion.

A. *The Liberal Interpretation*[30]

The principal argument for the extensive interpretation of canons 1892 and 1894 is based on canon 1680, § 2, which implies that an act is invalid if it depends on an invalid act. In the law on processes there are many formalities which are required under sanction of nullity of the acts of the case.[31] Consequently the sentence is, in virtue of canon 1680, § 2, invalid because of a derived nullity if it depends on an act which is invalid because of

---

[29] Crnica holds that neither the canons on the plaint of nullity nor the phrase *legis praescriptum* admit a liberal interpretation. He claims that the Code is therefore defective in that it offers no remedy for a sentence vitiated with a violation of procedural law which is not listed in canons 1892 and 1894.—"Defectus Codicis I.C. in designandis normis pro querela nullitatis." *Jus Pontificium,* XV (1935), 145-155.

[30] Roberti, *De Processibus,* II, nn. 491-494; 520, 523; idem, "Circa limites querelae nullitatis et restitutionis in integrum," *Apollinaris,* I (1928), 476-483; idem, "De nullitate sententiae ob defectum habilitatis ad accusandum matrimonium," *Apollinaris,* XII (1939), 415-416; idem, "De Nullitate Sententiate," *Apollinaris,* II (1929), 76-78; Hanssen, *De Sanctione Nullitatis in Processu Canonico,* pp. 155-156; Lemieux, *The Sentence in Ecclesiastical Procedure,* p. 99; Hogan, *Judicial Advocates and Procurators,* p. 169; Lega-Bartoccetti, *Commentarius,* II, 1022, 1025.

[31] Cf. *supra,* p. 188.

the violation of such a formality. It matters not whether the cause of the invalidity comes under one of the causes of nullity enumerated in canons 1892 and 1894. Moreover, violations of the natural law will invalidate the sentence for this same reason, and this position has been asserted several times by the Apostolic Signatura and the Roman Rota since the promulgation of the Code.[32]

The proponents of this opinion argue, too that there are other places in the Code where a demonstrative list appears to be all-inclusive. Thus the enumeration in canon 1902 of the cases which constitutes a *res iudicata* is not all-inclusive, for it fails to provide for cases of appeal in which there has intervened either an abatement or a renouncement;[33] yet in these cases the sentence of the first court becomes irrevocably adjudicated. Analogously, then, the lists in canons 1892 and 1894 are only demonstrative, since they do not provide for all the sentences which may be vitiated with a nullity which derives from invalid acts of procedure.[34]

Roberti employs an auxiliary argument in defense of his opinion, which argument involves even a greater controversy than the one under discussion; viz., whether or not the *restitutio in integrum* can be granted for a violation of procedural law. Roberti contends that it cannot. Consequently, a sentence which is vitiated for the reason that it depends on an invalid act of procedure that is not provided for in canons 1892 and 1894 cannot be remedied unless these canons are given a broad interpretation. If these canons are given a strict interpretation, such a sentence cannot be attacked with the complaint of nullity. Moreover, it cannot be opposed by the *restitutio in integrum,* for this is an extraordinary means to remedy injustice which results from a violation of substantive law.[35]

---

[32] Signatura: *De Manila* (Nullitatis et Restitutionis in Integrum seu Legati Pii), 6 apr. 1920—*AAS,* XII (1920), 256; Paderbornen (Nullitatis Matrimonii), 10 mart. 1919—*AAS,* XI (1919), 296, 297; S.R.R., *Mauranen. seu Camberien* (Nullitatis Sententiae), 13 iul. 1918, coram R.P.D. Ioanne Prior—*AAS,* XI (1919), 395. Cf. Roberti, *De Processibus,* II, nn. 493, 494; Hanssen, *op. cit.,* pp. 158, 163.

[33] Canons 1736-1739; 1740-1741.

[34] Roberti, *De Processibus,* II, n. 492.

[35] Roberti, *De Processibus,* II, n. 522; Hanssen, *op. cit.,* p. 159.

Roberti adduces very cogent arguments to prove that the ***restitution in integrum*** cannot be granted for violations of procedural law. He bases his reasons on the interpretation of the phrase, *"legis praescriptum evidenter neglectum,"* in canon 1905, § 2, 4°. It is sufficient for the present purpose to state, without reproducing his arguments, that Roberti contends that this phrase, because of the context in which it is found, refers only to violations of substantive law.[36] He concludes that the present legislation in the Code has completely separated errors in procedure from mistakes in judging, and that it has set down diverse remedies for them. The former give rise to the plaint of nullity. Consequently canons 1892 and 1894 are to be interpreted broadly. The latter are to be opposed by means of appeal or in extraordinary cases with the remedy of ***restitutio in integrum***.[37]

B. *The Strict Interpretation*

The opinion that a sentence can be invalid, at least in the sense that it can be opposed with the plaint of nullity, solely for the reasons which are listed in canons 1892 and 1894 has the numerical preponderance of authors in its favor.[38]

The principal arguments in defense of the strict interpretation are the following. The very text of the law of canons 1892 and 1894 allows only three causes of irremediable nullity and four causes of remediable nullity of the sentence. On the other hand, in virtue of canon 1905, § 2, 4°, the ***restitutio in integrum*** can be granted for a violation of formal procedural law. This remedy is allowed under certain conditions when injustice arises inasmuch

[36] Roberti, *De Processibus,* II, n. 522; Hanssen, *op. cit.,* p. 159.

[37] Roberti, *ibid.,* p. 262; Hanssen, *op. cit.,* p. 161.

[38] D'Angelo, "De Restitutione in Integrum," *Periodica de Religiosis et Missionariis* (Brugis, 1905-1919); *Periodica de Re Canonica et Morali Utili praesertim Religiosis et Missionariis* (Brugis, 1920-1927); *Periodica de Re Morali, Canonica, Liturgica* (Brugis, 1927-1936; Romae, 1937-), XVIII (1929), 37*-62* (hereafter cited *Periodica*); Wernz-Vidal, *Ius Canonicum,* VI, n. 623; Muñiz, *Procedimientos Eclésiasticos,* III, n. 505; Coronata, *Institutiones,* III, n. 1418; Crnica, "Defectus Codicis I.C. in designandis normis pro querelae nullitatis," *Ius Pontificium* (Romae, 1921-1940), XV (1935), 145-155; Feeney, *Restitutio in Integrum,* pp. 111-130.

as a prescript of law was evidently neglected in the course of the trial. The law does not distinguish between substantive and procedural law, so the invoking of a distinction seems unwarranted.[39]

The context bears out the fact that canons 1892 and 1894 contain all-inclusive lists. Canon 1893, which allows the plaint of nullity against an irremediably invalid sentence, states *"nullitas de qua in can. 1892 proponi potest"*; hence this canon indicates that the causes listed in canon 1892 are the only ones that furnish grounds for the plaint of irremediable nullity against the sentence. Likewise canon 1895 allows the plaint of remediable nullity *"in casibus de quibus in can. 1894"*; so only those reasons which are mentioned in canon 1894 render a sentence remediably null.[40]

The chief subsidiary argument for this opinion is based on the preparatory *Schemata* of the Code. Five of the progessive *Schemata* recognized as one of the grounds for the nullity of the sentence the fact that the sentence concluded a process that was invalid by reason of the violation of a law of precedure during the hearing of the case. In the *Schemata* this cause of invalidity was exemplified in an obviously demonstrative list of violations, for it read "Ipse processus vitio nullitatis est infestus, e.g. . . ."[41] This provision was present in *Schema G*, the last one to be drawn up before the Code; yet it was not included in canon 1892 or in canon 1894.[42] It is reasoned from this omission that the legislator intended that the sentence should be considered invalid only for a limited number of reasons, and that he by no means intended to set down a demonstrative list of the causes of invalidity of the sentence. Consequently, the listings in canons 1892 and 1894 are all-inclusive catalogues of the causes of nullity of the definitive sentence.[43]

It may be noted here that one of the desires expressed to the preparatory commission of the Code by the bishops was that the

---

[39] D'Angelo, *ibid.*, pp. 41*, 45*.

[40] Cf. Feeney, *Restitutio in Integrum*, p. 121.

[41] *Schemata*, F, can. 403, n. 5.

[42] *Schemata*, G, can. 388, n. 3. Cf. also *Schema B*, can. 297, n. 6; *Schema D*, can. 428, n. 5; *Schema E*, can. 449, n. 5.

[43] D'Angelo, "De Restitutione in Integrum," *Periodica*, XVIII (1929), 42*-44*.

number of the causes for granting the plaint of nullity be exhaustively defined.[44]

Another argument for this opinion is drawn from the sources of the law as set forth in the footnote of the Gasparri edition of the Code.[45] Too much stress should not be placed upon the citations contained in the footnotes of the Code; however, they demonstrate at least the interpretation placed on the canons by those responsible for the footnotes.[46] The notes set down in reference to canon 1892 allege only those sources which refer to the judge, the parties, and their procurators,[47] and the sources recorded for canon 1894 refer solely to the omission of the legitimate summons.[48]

On the other hand, the sources cited in the footnote to canon 1905, § 2, 4°, contains besides references to substantive law many examples of violations of procedural law. For example, cases cited from the Decretals include one in which the issue was not joined[49] another wherein the sentence was pronounced *"contra leges canonesque"*;[50] still another in which the prescribed order

---

[44] Roberti, "Codicis iuris canonici Schemata de processibus," *Acta Congressus Iuridici Internationalis 1934* (5 vols., Vol. IV, 1935, Romae: Apud Custodiam Librariam Pont. Instituti Utriusque Iuris), IV, 33.

[45] D'Angelo, "De Restitutione in Integrum," *Periodica*, XVIII (1929), 46*-48*.

[46] Serédi, "De valore iuridico fontium Codicis I.C.," *Jus Pontificium*, I (1921), 63-66.

[47] C. 41, C. II, q. 6; c. 22, X, *de officio et potestate iudicis delegati*, I, 29; c. 1, 3, 4, X, *de procuratoribus*, I, 38; c. 4, *de sententia et re iudicata*, II, 14, in VI°; Regulae servandae in iudiciis apud Suprem. Signaturae Ap. tribunal, 6 mart. 1912, Art. 4, c.—*AAS*, IV (1912), 189.

[48] C. 2, 4, 11, 12, C. III, q. 9; c. 10, X, *de sententia et re iudicata*, II, 27; c. 3, X, *ne sede vacante aliquid innovetur*, III, 9; S.C.C., *Lucana*, 2 et 16 dec. 1719 [*Fontes*, n. 3196]; *Albintimilien.*, 18 iun. 1746 [*Fontes*, n. 3586]; *Tranen*, 29 ian. 1859 [*Fontes*, n. 4172]; Lex propria S.R.Rotae et Signaturae Ap., 29 iun. 1908, can 32 § 3 [*Fontes*, n. 6459]; Regulae servandae in iudiciis apud S.R.Rotae Tribunal, 4 aug. 1910, § 182; [*Fontes*, n. 6461]; Regulae servandae in iudiciis apud Suprem. Signaturae Ap. Tribunal, 6 mart. 1912, Art. 4, a; Art. 5 [*Fontes*, n. 6462].

[49] C. 2, X, *ut lite non contestate non procedatur ad testium receptionem vel ad sententiam definitivam*, II, 6.

[50] C. 1, X, *de sententia et re iudicata*, II, 27.

for a trial was violated;[51] and there is also cited a case in which the sentence was pronounced on a day on which court could not be held.[52] The implication is that a sentence vitiated because of a violation of procedural law has a remedy in the *restitutio in integrum.*[53]

Only the very pertinent sources have been cited under canons 1892 and 1894. The other examples of invalid sentences in the earlier law have been transferred to the sources cited in the footnotes of the canon on the *restitutio in integrum.* From the arrangement of the footnotes of the canons under consideration, then, it is argued that the causes for nullity of the sentence have been reduced to a minimum, and that they are exhaustively listed in canons 1892 and 1894. If a sentence is vitiated with a cause other than one of those therein listed, it may be remedied through appeal, or, if the case warrants it, by means of the extraordinary remedy of the *restitutio in integrum.*[54]

The defenders of both sides of the controversy have had recourse to the jurisprudence of the Roman tribunals.[55] Most of the decisions cited by the proponents of the liberal interpretation of the canons on the plaint of nullity are pre-Code decisions.[56] Such decisions can have no bearing on the interpretation of the present law for the Rota has on several occasions noted that the law relative to invalidity in the sentence has changed.[57] Of the decisions handed down since the appearance of the Code, several seem to accept the liberal interpretation of the canons on the plaint

[51] C. 15, X, *de purgatione canonica,* V, 34.

[52] C. 5, X, *de feriis,* II, 9. Cf. also c. 9, X, *de sententia et re iudicata,* II, 27; Benedictus XIV, const. *Ad militantis,* 30 mart. 1742, § 43 [*Fontes,* n. 326]; S.C.C., *Premislien.,* 18 iun. 20 aug. 1887, ad 1 [*Fontes,* n. 4271]; Regulae servandae in iudiciis apud Suprem. Signaturae Ap. Tribunal, 6 mart. 1912, Art. 4, d, e [*Fontes,* n. 6462].

[53] D'Angelo, "De Restitutione in Integrum," *Periodica,* XVIII (1929), 48*.

[54] D'Angelo, *ibid.,* pp. 45*, 46*, 48*; cf. Wernz-Vidal, *Ius Canonicum,* VI, n. 623.

[55] D'Angelo, *ibid.,* pp. 60*, 61*.

[56] Cf. Hanssen, *De Sanctione Nullitatis in Processu Canonico,* p. 163.

[57] *S. Iacobi de Chile* (Restitutionis in Integrum et Compromissi), 5 iul. 1927; coram R.P.D. Francisco Parrillo, dec. XXXIV, n. 4—*Decisiones,* XIX (1927), 278; cf. also *Decisiones,* XI (1919), 76 ff.

of nullity. There are two decisions of the Signatura which indicate that a sentence may be invalid for reasons other than those stated in canons 1892 and 1894.[58] It must be remembered that the Signatura still acts, as it has expressly asserted, according to its own *Regulae* as interpreted by the Chirograph of Benedict XV.[59] In fact, the Signatura seemed to admit the all-inclusive nature of the lists in canons 1892 and 1894, when it expressly declared itself not bound by the limits of those canons.[60]

Monsignor D'Angelo referred to only two Rota decisions.[61] Since his death in 1930 there have been published Rota decisions which espouse his opinion, and which definitely established the precedent for the interpretation of canons 1892 and 1894 which states that these canons contain all-inclusive lists of the causes of nullity in the definitive sentence. The doctrine contained in these decisions which justifies the conclusion will be set forth in the discussion which follows.

C. *The Jurisprudence of the Sacred Roman Rota*

The post-Code decisions of the Rota agree that the present legislation has quite drastically changed the provisions of the old law in regard to the cases in which the plaint of nullity is allowed and in reference to the grounds for which the *restitutio in*

---

[58] *Paderbornen.* (Nullitatis Matrimonii), 31 maii 1919—*AAS,* XI (1919), 297; *De Manila* (*Nullitatis et Restitutionis in Integrum*), 6 apr. 1920—*AAS,* XII (1920), 256.

[59] Benedictus XV, chirographum *Attentis expositis,* 28 iun. 1915 (*Appendix ad regulas servandas in iudictis apud Suprem. Signaturae Ap. Tribunal,* Art. 1)—*AAS,* VII (1915), 320-325.

[60] (*Sententiae incidentalis*), "Et quidem, in vim eiusdem Chirographi competentia huius S.T. circa nullitatem sententiarum S.R. Rotae, non coarctatur limitibus can. 1892 et 1894 signatis; recursus enim quoque admittitur si lata sententia sit manifesto vel contra legem vel non satis perpensa factorum veritate. Et haec latior competentia patet ex Regulis huius S.T. (Art. 4) et ex earum appendice (Art. 1). . . ."—*AAS,* XV (1923), 183. *Romana,* 25 nov. 1922.

[61] S.R.R., *Restitutionis in integrum,* 8 apr. 1919—*Decisiones,* XI (1919), 76-87; *S. Iacobi de Chile* (Restitutionis in Integrum et Compromissi), 5 iul. 1927, dec. XXXIV—*Decisiones,* XIX (1927), 276 sqq; D'Angelo, *ibid.,* p. 60*, 61*.

integrum may be granted. In one decision handed down in 1927 in a case from Santiago, Chile, the Rota completely accepted the interpretation of D'Angelo of the term *legis praescriptum* in canon 1905, § 2, 4°. It employed some of his arguments verbatim.[62]

In the discussion of this case the panel of auditors adverted to three points: 1.) that the old law has in part been changed;[63] 2.) that the *restitutio in integrum* can be granted for a violation of procedural law.[64] 3.) that the number of reasons for nullity in the definitive sentence have been reduced to only those that are mentioned in canons 1892 and 1894.[65] This last point is set down as if there could be no questioning its truth. The auditors in this case indicated that it was the mind of the legislator to curtail the number of the reasons for nullity, and that the Code accomplished this purpose by reducing the number of the reasons for substantial and irremediable nullity in the definitive sentence to three, and by admitting as reasons for remediable nullity only those that are listed in canon 1894.[66] By this legislation the Code solved a problem that had grown to enormous proportions in the earlier law.[67]

In deciding a case in 1933 the Rota *ex professo* treated of the

---

[62] S.R.R., *S. Iacobi de Chile* (Restitutionis in Integrum et Compromissi), 5 iul. 1927, coram R.P.D. Francisco Parrillo, dec. XXXIV, nn. 4-11—*Decisiones,* XIX (1927), 276 sqq.

[63] ". . . Cum autem codex veterem disciplinam hac in re nonnihil novaverit."—*Ibid.,* n. 4, p. 278.

[64] "Ne autem praescripta legum . . . impune a iudicibus violari et negligi possent, voluit [Codex] ea opportune remedio communire, non quidem nullitatis, prout antiqua iure eveniebat, sed restitutionis in integrum."—*Ibid.,* n. 6, p. 280. A Rota decision in 1935 explained that the canonists have not uniformly interpreted the phrase, *"legis praescriptum evidenter neglectum,"* and that no safe norm could be deduced from jurisprudence in this matter; however, until the Pontifical Commission for the Authentic Interpretation of the Code decreed otherwise, the word "law" in canon 1905, § 2, 4°, was to be taken without modification. It included all law, both that which referred to the merits of the case and also that which regulated the manner of procedure. S.R.R., *Restitutionis in Integrum,* II apr. 1935, coram R.P.D. Arcturo Wynen, dec. XXV, n. 7—*Decisiones,* XXVIII (1935), 221.

[65] *Ibid.,* nn. 6, 11, 13, pp. 280, 283, 284.

[66] *Ibid.,* n. 6, p. 280.

[67] ". . . voluit quidem nullitatis capita resecare, quae veteri iure longe patebant."—*Ibid.,* n. 13, p. 284.

reasons for invalidity in the definitive sentence, and expressly declared that the lists of defects which in canons 1892 and 1894 vitiate the sentence with remediable or irremediable nullity are all-inclusive.[68] The case was that of a priest who had been tried on a criminal charge before the metropolitan tribunal of Madrid, and later before the metropolitan tribunal of Toledo. The Rota declared the sentence of the tribunal of Toledo invalid in virtue of the provision of canon 1894, 1°, which states that a sentence is remediably null when there has not been any legal summons. Since this was a criminal trial, the promoter of justice had an essential part in the trial and should have been duly summoned. The Rota very carefully pointed out that it was not in virtue of canon 1587, § 2, that the sentence was invalid. It granted that by this canon the judicial acts of certain trials if performed without the intervention of the promoter of justice are invalid, but it definitely stated that the sentence is not on that account invalid.[69]

In this case the Rota gives a precise explanation of the relationship between the invalid acts of a trial and the sentence that concludes such a trial: An invalid sentence does not always and necessarily result from invalid acts of procedure. As a matter of fact, the grounds for an invalid sentence are specifically designated in the law, and the judge does not have the power, in adverse matters such as this, to extend the law to cover other analogous cases. When the law declares acts invalid inasmuch as they were executed without the intervention of a certain person or without the observance of certain solemnities which are required under sanction of nullity, it does not intend that the sentence which is based on these acts should be pronounced; rather it intends that in due time the parties should provide for the declaration of the nullity of those acts, and that they should also bring about their valid renewal of them. Should the judge pronounce a sentence that is based on invalid acts, this sentence cannot be opposed by means

---

[68] S.R.R., *Matriten* (Nullitatis Actorum et Sententiae), 3 iul. 1933, coram R.P.D. Francisco Parrillo, dec. XLVIII, n. 2—*Decisiones,* XXV (1933), 420-423.

[69] ". . . acta quidem sunt nulla (can. 1587, § 2), haud vero semper sententia, quae super his actis nullis fuerit forte prolata."—*Ibid.,* n. 3, p. 421.

of the complaint of nullity unless the invalid procedural acts come under one of the heads which are exhaustively designated in the law as reasons for the remediable or irremediable nullity in the sentence. When none of these reasons is verified, the sentence cannot be declared null. But it may possibly be rescinded through use of the extraordinary remedy of the *restitutio in integrum* in virtue of canon 1905, § 2, 4°, which allows this remedy for an evident neglect or violation of a precept of law.[70]

In a matrimonial case in 1934 the Rota decided that the respective sentences of the tribunals of Paris and Versailles were valid even though many of the acts of the tribunal of Paris had been invalid, mainly in consequence of the fact that several witnesses had been questioned by the tribunal of Paris without the presence of a notary or of the defender of the bond. Reference was made in this case to canon 11, which states that one is to regard as invalidating or disqualifying only those laws which expressly or equivalently state that an action is null and void, or that a person is incapacitated to place a valid act. Consequently, under the present legislation no other nullities of sentence at all are to be admitted except those which are exhaustively listed in canons 1892 and 1894.[71]

More recent decisions of the Rota can also be cited in favor of the strict interpretation of the canons under discussion. In 1936 there was decided a case in which many provisions of procedural law had been either neglected or omitted. Nevertheless, the sentence was invalid only in the manner of a remediable nullity, that is, for the failure to summon the defendant.[72]

In that same year the Rota decided that the sentence of the second instance in another case was invalid only because the dedendant had not been summoned. The other reasons for the invalidity of the sentence were not admitted. They were the absence

---

[70] *Ibid.*, n. 2, p. 421.

[71] S.R.R., *Parisien* (Nullitatis Matrimonii), 7 iun. 1934, coram R.P.D. Henrico Quattrocalo, dec. XL, nn. 6, 7—*Decisiones,* XXVI (1934), 349, 350.

[72] S.R.R., *Querelae Nullitatis et Nullitatis Matrimonii,* 8 febr. 1936, coram R.P.D. Andrea Jullien, dec. XII, n. 6—*Decisiones,* XXVIII (1936), 119.

of the defender of the bond; the counsel of the presiding judge to the other collegiate judges to render their decisions before the closing of the case; and the rejection of some witnesses who had been introduced by the plaintiff, though he had not been permitted to seek redress against this act. In the decision of this case the Rota reiterated the jurisprudence of a former sentence,[73] which had stated that the Code has curtailed the number of the reasons for nullity in a sentence and had reduced them to those which receive mention in canons 1892 and 1894. The decision of 1936 also remarked that the complaint of nullity cannot be used except for one of the reasons enumerated in the aforesaid canons.[74]

A very interesting decision was handed down by the Rota in 1937. In this decision the Rota declared that the sentence of the tribunal of Reggio-Calabria in a matrimonial case was invalid on the grounds that it was a prejudicial attempt against the rights of the plaintiff. At first sight this decision seems to militate against the strict interpretation of the canons on the plaint of nullity, but, as will be seen, it rather strongly confirms this opinion.

In the first instance of the trial in the tribunal of Reggio-Cababria, after the closing of the case and the presentation of the defense and the responses of the defender of the bond, the plaintiff's advocate resigned. A newly-appointed advocate requested that the case be reopened inasmuch as other witnesses and more evidence had been discovered. His petition was rejected in a decree of the judge, and forthwith he duly appealed against this decree. Notwithstanding this appeal the tribunal proceeded to pronounce the definitive sentence, which upheld the validity of the marriage.

When the case came before the Sacred Roman Rota, the Rota declared that, since the appeal had been from a decree or an interlocutory sentence which had definitive force, inasmuch as it had an immediate bearing on the final sentence, the jurisdiction of the

---

[73] S.R.R., *S. Iacobi de Chile* (Restitutionis in Integrum et Compromissi), 5 iul. 1927, coram R.P.D. Francisco Parrillo, dec. XXXIV, n. 6—*Decisiones,* XIX (1927), 280.

[74] S.R.R., *Tergestina* (Querelae Nullitatis et Nullitatis Matrimonii), 22 oct. 1936, coram R.P.D. Arcturo Wynen, dec. LXV, n. 2—*Decisiones,* XXVIII (1936), 621 sqq.

judiciary was suspended until the appeal was prosecuted in virtue of the principle, *"lite pendente, nihil innovetur."* For that tribunal to proceed with the case and to pronounce the definitive sentence was to constitute a prejudicial attempt against the plaintiff's right of appeal. Consequently, this action of the tribunal was, according to canon 1855, *ipso iure* invalid. The Rota was careful to point out that it was not so much the sentence as the prejudicial attempt that was declared invalid. Not only was the sentence null and void, but also all the acts which that tribunal had executed relative to the case since the day that the advocate had interposed the appeal were without juridic effect. The Rota pointed out that this case could not be decided on the principle of the plaint of nullity as warranted in canons 1892-1895, since these canons do not admit prejudicial attempts as grounds for the use of that remedy.[75] Hence the Rota decision again favored the opinion that the lists of the reasons for invalidity in the definitive sentence which are contained in canons 1892 and 1894 are all-inclusive. The following year another *turnus* of the Rota confirmed this decision.[76]

In the light of the clear and repeated statements in the decisions of the Sacred Roman Rota with regard to the invalidity of the definitive sentence, the opinion which favors the liberal interpretation of the canons on the plaint of nullity is hardly tenable. The Rota has definitely established a precedent in this regard. Such a precedent does indeed not have the force of law, neither for the Rota nor for other tribunals, but it has a certain intrinsic authority in view of the solid jurisprudence upon which it is based. Consequently to ignore such a precedent would be to act rashly and contrary to the best doctrinal interpretation of the law.[77]

---

[75] "Unde dubium propositum sub principiis de attentatis est definiendum, non vero de querela nullitatis, quae ad normam cann. 1892-1895 non apud nostrum Tribunal sed apud illud a quo sententia lata est esset proponenda, et ceteroquin tantum ob aliquod ex capitibus ibidem expressis."—S.R.R., *Rhegingen.* (Nullitatis Matrimonii Incidentis), 16 iul. 1937, coram R.P.D. Ioanne Teadori, dec. LI, n. 6—*Decisiones,* XXIX (1937), 514.

[76] S.R.R., *Rheginen.* (Nullitatis Matrimonii Incidentis), 28 iul. 1938, coram R.P.D. Guillelmo Heard, dec. LI—*Decisiones,* XXX (1938), 472-477.

[77] Cf. Cardinal Lega's statement: "De auctoritate collectionum decisionum rotalium sufficiat advertere has non habere auctoritatem *extrinsecam seu* collatam ab eo qui vim legis tribuere valet prouti factum est de Collectionibus

In at least seven different decisions the Rota has indicated that the listings in canons 1892 and 1894 are all-inclusive catalogues of the reasons for nullity in the definitive sentence. That the Rotal jurisprudence should espouse this opinion is certainly in accord with the letter and the spirit of the present legislation, which is to reduce invalid actions, invalid sentences, and all other forms of invalidity to a minimum.[78]

Moreover, a careful analysis of Roberti's arguments will reveal that his contention—that the lists in canons 1892 and 1894 are not all-inclusive—has not been sufficiently demonstrated. Canon 1680 does allow that an act may be null because of a derived nullity, but this general law is limited by the particular canons on the plaint of nullity.

His argument, too, that there are other places in the Code where a list only appears to be all-inclusive, can be attacked in virtue of the very canon which he cites as an example. He says that, though canon 1902 seems to completely list the cause of the *res iudicata,* it does not provide for the abatement and renouncement of a case on appeal. In reality it does, for these causes readily fall into the category of the deserted appeal, which is specifically listed in canon 1902, 2°.[79]

As a matter of fact, a comparison of the canons on the plaint of nullity with evidently demonstrative lists in the Code rather shows that these canons do contain exhaustive lists. For instance, canon 1813, § 1, in giving examples of public documents states: "The principal public ecclesiastical documents are these. . . ." Canon 2147, § 2, in noting the reasons for the removal of an irremovable pastor states "These causes are especially the ones which follow.

Decretalium. Habent tamen auctoritatem *intrinsecam* seu attributam in scholis et in foro ob solidissimam iurisprudentiam unde dictae sunt magistrales. Id fatentur unanimi sententia iuris communis interpretes qui etiam ratam habent et confirmant sententiam Emerix, nempe decisiones rotales praevalere communi opinioni."—*Coram Lega Habitae S.R. Rotae Decisiones sive Sententiae quas nempe Emus Cardinalis Michael Lega annis 1909-1914 eiusdem Sacri Auditorii Decanus exaravit* (2. ed., Romae: Typis Polyglottis Vaticanis, 1926), Praefatio, p. 63, n. 57.

[78] Cf. canons 11; 1680.

[79] Cf. canons 1736-1738; 1740; 1741; Feeney, *Restitutio in Integrum,* p. 122.

. . ." In other canons the use of the sign *"etc."* clearly indicates a demonstrative list, e.g., in canons 1629, § 1, and 1642, § 1. If the legislator wished to give a merely demonstrative list of the causes of invalid sentences, he should have included in the canon some general statement like the one which was proposed in the preliminary draft of the Code, viz., that a sentence is invalid when it concludes a process that is infected with nullity, e.g. . . .[80]

It must be pointed out also that Roberti's opinion allows too much liberty to the individual judge. The question as to which violations of procedural law, other than those which are listed in canons 1892 and 1894, will render a sentence invalid, and whether the nature of the nullity will be remediable or irremediable will not be beyond dispute. As was previously noted, the Rota has remarked that this liberty is not granted to the individual judge, since the grounds for invalid sentences are specifically designated in the law, and the judge, since there is question of a *res odiosa,* does not have the power to extend the law to cover analogous cases.[81]

Roberti's argument—that in consequence of the strict interpretation it may sometimes happen that there will be no remedy for a sentence which is defective as the result of a violation of procedural law—cannot go unchallenged. In some cases the ordinary remedy of appeal will furnish sufficient redress. Moreover, in other cases wherein grave injustice has resulted, the *restitutio in integrum* is made available. The Rota has granted this remedy for a violation of procedural law.[82]

In view of the pre-Code experience with judicial nullity and the danger of an exaggerated formalism which is latent in an unnecessary preoccupation with the letter of the law, the jurisprudence which establishes the strict interpretation of the canons on the plaint of nullity should be enthusiastically welcomed.

---

[80] *Schemata,* F, can. 403, n. 5; Crnica, "Defectus Codicis I.C. in designandis normis pro querela nullitatis," *Jus Pontificium,* XV (1935), 148-149.

[81] S.R.R., *Matriten.* (Nullitatis Actorum et Sententiae), 3 iul. 1933, coram R.P.D. Francisco Parrillo, dec. XLVII, n. 2—*Decisiones,* XXV (1933), 421.

[82] S.R.R., *S. Iacobi de Chile* (Restitutionis in Integrum et Compromissi), 5 iul. 1927, coram R.P.D. Francisco Parrillo, dec. XXIV—*Decisiones,* XIX (1927), 276 sqq.

CONCLUSIONS

Gathered here in summary are more important particular conclusions arrived at in this study on the question of nullity in judicial acts. Some of them were selected because in the light of new considerations they seem to be the better opinions of disputed questions.

1. The law of the Code has drastically reduced the number of the reasons for judicial nullity, and thereby has corrected a problem that had grown to enormous proportions in the pre-Code law.

2. In view of the intent of the Code to reduce the reasons for judicial nullity to a minimum, in cases of doubt the presumption will be decidedly in favor of the validity of the act in question.

3. Acts executed by a judge the while there is still pending the settlement of the exception of suspicion which has been raised against him are *ipso iure* invalid.

4. Except on the extraordinary occasions mentioned in canon 1637, when the law prorogues a local judge's jurisdiction he is absolutely incompetent in the invalidating sense of canon 1892, 1°, for exercising judicial power outside the territorial limits of his jurisdiction.

5. The juridic capacity and the procedural capacity of the litigants affect the validity of the trial, but the laws which control the proper qualification of the litigants, namely, their legitimation to act in a certain case, are not all invalidating laws.

6. An unbaptized person ordinarily lacks the right to stand in judgment in an ecclesiastical court in the invalidating sense of canon 1892, 2°.

7. Merely private pious associations or institutions, though they are not constituted as moral persons, may sue or be sued in church courts.

8. The unauthorized representations in court of moral persons, or of physical persons who are deprived of the free administration of their goods, vitiates the sentence, with irremediable nullity, since

such representation remains minus the right for the representative to stand in judgment.

9. Excommunicated persons do not lack the right to stand in judgment in the invalidating sense of canon 1892, 2° ; nor do apostates, heretics and schismatics.

10. The mandate of a procurator is invalid if it does not meet the specifications of canon 1659.

11. The absence of a formal bill of complaint does not nullify the trial.

12. The canons which control the legitimate serving of the summons, and which consequently affect the validity of the summons are canons 1713, 1717, 1719, 1720, but not canon 1721.

13. For citations other than the initial summons of the defendant, if the regulations which govern legal summonses are observed in substance, such citations will not be invalid, since the law permits that the formalities be adapted to the diverse nature of the acts for which a summons is required.

14. It is the omission of the initial summons of the defendant, and not that of the summons to the session for the publication of the sentence, that renders the definitive sentence remediably null.

15. The occurrence of invalid acts in the course of the trial does not necessarily invalidate the definitive sentence.

16. The lists of the causes of irremediable nullity in canon 1892 and of remediable nullity in canon 1894 are all-inclusive catalogues. No other reasons furnish grounds for the granting of the plaint of nullity.

17. By reducing the number of reasons for nullity in the definitive sentence, the lawgiver does not imply that valid sentences may be based upon invalid acts of procedure. Rather, when invalid acts of procedure other than those referred to in canons 1892 and 1894 occur in the course of the trial, the invalidity should be remedied by means of a renewal of the act in due time. If it is not remedied, and if as a consequence grave injustice befalls a litigant, then there appear to be grounds for a *restitutio in integrum*.

BIBLIOGRAPHY

Sources

Acta Apostolica Sedis, Commentarium Officiale, Romae, 1909.

Bouscaren, T. Lincoln, *The Canon Law Digest, Officially Published Documents Affecting the Code of Canon Law,* 2 vols., Milwaukee: The Bruce Publishing Company, 1934-1943.

Bruns, H. Th., *Canones Apostolorum et Conciliorum Saeculorum,* IV-VII, 2 vols., Berolini, Reimeri, 1839.

Bullarum Diplomatum et Privilegiorum Sanctorum Romanorum Pontificum Taurinensis Editio, 24 vols. et Appendix, Augustae Tautrinorum, Neapoli, 1857-1872.

Codicis Iuris Canonici Fontes cura Em̃i Petri Card. Gasparri editi, 9 vols., Romae (postea Civitate Vaticana): Typis Polyglottis Vaticanis, 1923-1939 (Vols. VII-IX ed. cura et studio Em̃i Iustiniani Card. Serédi).

Coram Lega Habitae S. R. Rotae Decisiones sive Sententiae quas nempe Em̃us Cardinalis Michael Lega annis 1909-1914 eiusdem Sacri Auditorii Decanus exaravit, 2. ed., Romae: Typis Polyglottis Vaticanis, 1926.

Corpus Iuris Canonici, 2. ed., Lipsiensis, post Aemilii Ludovici Richteri curas instruxit Aemilius Friedberg, 2 vols., Lipsiae, 1879-1881. Editio anastatice refetita, 1922.

Corpus Iuris Civilis, Vol. I, *Institutiones,* ed. stereotypa 15. recognovit P. Krueger; Vol. X, *Digesta,* ed. stereotypa 15. recognovit T. Mommsen, retractavit P. Krueger; Vol. II, *Codex Iustinianus,* ed. stereoptypa 10. recognovit et retractavit P. Krueger; Vol. III, *Novellae Constitutiones,* ed. stereoptypa 5. R. Schoell; opus Schoelli morte interceptum absolvit G. Kroll, Berolini: apud Weidmannos, 1928-1929.

Corpus Iuris Civilis, 5 vols., Lugduni, 1553-1557.

Decretales D. Gregorii IX, una cum Glossis Restitutae, Romae, 1582.

Decretum Gratiani emendatum et notationibus illustratum, una cum glossis, Gregorii XIII Pont. Max. iussu editum, 2 vols., Romae, 1582.

Jaffé, P., *Regesta Pontificum Romanorum ab condita Ecclesia ad annum post Christum natum MCXCVIII,* 2. ed. correctam et auctam suspiciis Gulielmi Wattenbach curaverunt S. Loewenfeld, F. Kaltenbrunner, P. Ewald, 2 vols., Lipsiae, 1885-1888.

Liber Sextus Decretalium D. Bonifacii Papae VIII suae integritati una cum Clementinis et Extravagantibus earumque Glossis restitutus, Romae, 1582.

Mansi, Joannes, *Sacrorum Conciliorum Nova et Amplissima Collectio,* 53 vols. in 60, Parisiis, 1901-1927.

Monumenta Germaniae Historica, Gregorii I Papae, Registrum Epistularum, Tomus I et II, ediderunt P. Ewald et L. Hartmann, Berolini: Apud Weidmannos, 1891-1899.

Potthast, A., *Regesta Pontificum Romanorum inde ab anno post Christum natum MCXCVIII ad annum MCCCIV,* 2 vols., Berolini, 1874-1875.

Sacrae Romanae Rotae Decisiones seu Sententiae (ab anno 1909), Romae: Typis Vaticanis, 1912-

Schroeder, H. J., *Disciplinary Decrees of the General Councils,* St. Louis: Herder, 1937.

Reference Works

Acta Congressus Iuridici Internationalis, 1934, 5 vols., 1935-1937, Vol. IV, 1935, Romae: Apud Custodiam Librariam Pont. Instituti Utriusque Iuris.

Altimarus, Blasius, *Tractatus de Nullitatibus in XIV Rubricas Divisus,* Neapoli, 1678.

American Jurisprudence, by the editorial staff of the publishers, Vol. II, Rochester, New York: The Lawyers Cooperative Publishing Company, 1936.

Augustine, Charles, *A Commentary on the New Code of Canon Law,* 8 vols., Vol. VII, 3. ed., 1930, St. Louis, Mo.: B. Herder & Co.

Bartolus a Saxoferrato, *Commentaria,* Tomus VIII, *In Secundum atque Tertiam Codicis Partem,* Venetiis, 1590.

Berutti, Christophorus, *Institutiones Iuris Canonici,* 6 vols., Vol. II, Pars I, Taurini-Romae: Marietti, 1943.

Beste, Udalricus, *Introductio in Codicem,* 3. ed., Collegeville, Minn.: St. John's Abbey Press, 1946.

Blackstone, W., *Commentaries on the Laws of England,* 4. ed. by James DeWith Andrews, 4 vols. in 2, Chicago: Callaghan and Company, 1899.

Blat, Albertus, *Commentarium Textus Codicis Iuris Canonici, Liber IV, De Processibus,* Romae: Collegio Angelico, 1927.

Bouix, D., *Tractatus de Judiciis Ecclesiasticis,* 2. ed., 2 vols., Pariis, 1866.

Burke, Thomas J., *Competence in Ecclesiastical Tribunals,* The Catholic University of America Canon Law Studies, n. 14; Washington, D. C.: The Catholic University of America, 1922.

Cappello, Felix, *Summa Iuris Canonici,* Vol. III, editio altera emendata et aucta, Romae: Apud Aedes Universitatis Gregorianae, 1940.

Chelodi, Ioannes, *Ius Canonicum de Personis,* 3. ed., curavit P. Ciprotti, Trento: Libreria Moderna Editrice, 1942.

Cocchi, Guidus, *Commentarium in Codicem Iuris Canonici,* 8 vols. in 5, Vol. VII, *De Processibus,* 3. ed., 1940, Taurinorum Augustae: Marietti.

Connolly, Thomas, *Appeals,* The Catholic University of America Canon Law Studies, n. 79, Washington, D. C.: The Catholic University of America, 1932.

Coronata, Matthaeus Conte a, *Institutiones Iuris Canonici,* 5 vols., Romae: Marietti. Vols. I-IV editio altera aucta et emendata, Vols. I-II, 1939; Vol. III, 1941; Vol. IV, 1945; Vol. V, 1936.

De Luca, J. B., *Theatrum Veritatis et Justitiae,* 16 vols. in 9, Coloniae Agrippinae, 1706.

De Meester, Alphonsus, *Juris Canonici et Juris Canonico-Civilis Compendium,* nova editio, 3 vols., in 4, Brugis: Desclee De Brouwer, 1921-1928.

Doheny, William J., *Canonical Procedure in Matrimonial Cases,* Vol. I, *Formal Judicial Procedure,* 2. ed., Milwaukee: The Bruce Publishing Company, 1948.

Durandus, Gulielmus, *Speculum Iuris,* 3 vols., Venetiis, 1577.

Eichmann, Eduard, *Das Prozessrecht des Codex Iuris Canonici,* Paderborn, 1921.

———, *Lehrbuch des Kirchenrechts auf Grund des Codex Iuris Canonici,* 2. ed., Paderborn: Ferdinand Schoningh, 1926.

Engel, L., *Collegium Universi Iuris Canonici,* ed. nova, post omnes alias recognita et Locupleta, cui nunc primum adjectae sunt annotationes Gaspari Barthel, Beneventi, 1760.

Engelmann, Arthur, and Others, *A History of Continental Civil Procedure,* Vol. VII of *The Continental Legal History Series*—published under the Association of American Law Schools, Boston: Little, Brown and Company, 1927.

Feney, Thos., *Restitutio in Integrum,* The Catholic University of America Canon Law Studies, n. 129, Washington, D. C.: The Catholic University of America Press, 1941.

Gasparri, Patrus, *Tractatus Canonicus de Matrimonio,* ed. nova ad mentem Codicis I.C., 2 vols., Typis Polyglottis Vaticanis, 1932.

Gonzalez-Tellez, Manuel, *Commentaria Perpetua in singulos textus quinque librorum Decretalium Gregorii IX,* 5 vols., Venetiis, 1756.

Hanssen, Antonius, *De Sanctione Nullitatis in Processu Canonico,* Romae: Apollinaris, 1939.

Hogan, James, *Judicial Advocates and Procurators,* The Catholic University of America Canon Law Studies, n. 133, Washington, D. C.; The Catholic University of America Press, 1941.

Hostiensis, Card. (Henricus de Segusio), *Summa Aurea,* Venetiis, 1568.

Ioannes Andreae, *In Quinque Decretalium Libros Novella Commentaria,* 4 vols., Venetiis, 1581.

Kealy, John, *The Introductory Libellus in Church Court Procedure,* The Catholic University of America Canon Law Studies, n. 108, Washington, D. C.: The Catholic University of America, 1937.

Kilcullen, Thomas J., *The Collegiate Moral Person as Party Litigant,* The Catholic University of America Canon Law Studies, n. 251, Washington, D. C.: The Catholic University of America Press, 1947.

Król, John J., *The Defendant in Contentious Trials,* The Catholic University of America Canon Law Studies, n. 146, Washington, D. C.: The Catholic University of America Press, 1942.

Lega, Michael Card. *Praelectiones in Textum Iuris Canonici de Iudiciis Ecclesiasticis in Scholis Pont. Sem. Rom. Habitae,* 4 vols., Romae, 1896-1901.

———, -Bartoccetti, V., *Commentarius in Iudicia Ecclesiastica iuxta Codicem Iuris Canonici,* 3 vols., Romae: Anonima Libraria Cattolica Italiana, 1938-1941.

Lemieux, Delisle, *The Sentence in Ecclesiastical Procedure,* The Catholic University of America Canon Law Studies, n. 87, Washington, D. C.: The Catholic University of America, 1934.

Maranta, Robertus, *Speculum Aurem et Lumen Advocatorum Praxis Civilis;* Venetiis, 1590.

Maroto, Philippus, *Institutiones Iuris Canonici,* 2 vols., Matriti, 1918-1919.

Muñiz, T., *Procedimientos Eclesiásticos,* 2. ed., 3 vols., Seville: Lib. de Sobrino de Izquierdo, 1926.

Noval, J., *Commentarium Codicis Iuris Canonici,* Lib. IV, *De Processibus,* Pars I, *De Iudiciis,* Augustae Taurinorum; Marietti, 1920.

Ottaviani, Alaphridus, *Institutiones Iuris Publici Ecclesiastici,* Vol. I, *Ius Publicum Internum,* 3. ed., Romae: Typis Polyglottis Vaticanis, 1948.

Panormitanus (Nicholaus de Tudeschis), *Commentaria in Quinque Libros Decretalium,* 5 vols. in 7, Venetiis, 1588.

Pellegrini, Carolus, *Praxis Vicariorum et Omnium in Utroque Foro Iusdicentium,* Venetiis, 1706.

Pichler, Vitus, *Ius Canonicum secundum quinque Decretalium titulos Gregorii Papae IX practice explicatum,* 2 vols., Ravennae, 1741.

Pirhing, Ernricus, *Jus Canonicum in V Libros Decretalium,* ed. novissima, 4 vols., Dilingae, 1722.

Pollock, F., and Maitland, F. W., *The History of English Law before the time of Edward I,* 2 vols., Boston: Little, Brown and Company, 1895.

Prümmer, Dominicus, *Manuale Iuris Canonici,* 6. ed., Friburgi Brisgoviae: Herder, 1933.

Regatillo, E., *Institutiones Iuris Canonici,* 2 vols., Santander: Sal Terrae, 1941-1942.

Reiffenstuel, Anacletus, *Jus Canonicum Universum,* 5 vols. in 7, Parisiis, 1864-1870.

Roberti, Franciscus, *Codicis Iuris Canonici Schemata,* Lib. IV, *De Processibus,* Romae: Typis Polyglottis Vaticanis, 1940.

———, *De Processibus,* 2 vols., Romae: Apud Aedes Facultates Iuridicae ad S. Apollinaris, 1926.

———, *De Processibus,* Vol. I, 2. ed., Romae: Apud Custodiam Librariam Pontificii Instituti Utriusque Iuris, 1941.

Schmalzgrueber, Franciscus, *Jus Ecclesiasticum Universum,* 5 vols. in 12, Romae, 1843-1845.

Schmier, Franciscus, *Ius Canonicum Universum*, Venetiis, 1754.

Tobin, Thomas J., *De Officiali Curiae Dioecesanae*, Romae: Apud Aedes Pontificiae Universitatis Gregorianae, 1936.

Toso, Albertus, *Ad Codicem Iuris Canonici . . . Commentaria Minora*, Lib. II, Tom. I, Taurini-Romae: Marietti, 1922.

Van Hove, A., *Commentarium Lovaniense in Codicem Iuris Canonici*, Vol. I, Tom. I, *Prolegomena*, 2. ed., Mechliniae et Romae: H. Dessain, 1945.

Vantius, Sebastianus, *Tractatus de Nullitatibus Processuum et Sententiarum*, Venetiis: Apud Jacobum Cornettum, 1588.

Vermeersch, Arthurus-Creusen, Josephus, *Epitome Iuris Canonici*, 3 vols., 6. ed., Mechliniae-Romae: H. Dessain, 1937-1946.

Wernz, Franciscus, *Ius Decretalium*, 2. ed., 6 vols., Romae et Prati, 1906-1913.

Wernz, F. X.-Vidal, P., *Ius Canonicum*, Vol. VI, *De Processibus*, Romae: Apud Aedes Universitatis Gregorianae, 1927.

Woywod, S., *A Practical Commentary on the Code of Canon Law*, Revised and enlarged edition by Callistus Smith, 2 vols., New York: Joseph F. Wagner, Inc., 1948.

Articles

Cappello, Felix, "De acatholicorum incapacitate agendi in foro ecclesiastico," *Miscellanea Vermeersch*, 2 vols., Romae: Pontificia Universita Gregoriana, 1935, I, 393-402.

Crnica, A., "Defectus Codicis in designandis normis pro querela nullitatis," *Jus Pontificium*, XV (1935), 145-155.

D'Angelo, Sosio, "De restitutione in integrum iuxta canonem 1905, § 2, 4°, *Periodica*, XVIII (1929), 37*-62*.

Hanssen, Antonius, "De sanctione nullitatis in processu canonico," *Apollinaris*, XI (1923), 71-109; 215-263; 381-403; XII (1939), 198-251.

Ramos, D., "De conditione saecularium in domibus religiosorum," *Commentarium pro Religiosis*, VI (1925), 28-32; 82-86; 136-140; 187-190; 324-329; 479-483.

Roberti, F., "Circa limites querelae nullitatis et restitutionis in integrum," *Apollinaris*, I (1928), 476-483.

———, "Codicis Iuris Canonici schemata de processibus," *Acta Congressus Iuridici Internationalis, 1934*, 5 vols., Vol. IV (1935), 33.

———, "De nullitate sententiae ob defectum habilitatis ad accusandum matrimonium," *Apollinaris*, XII (1939), 415-416.

———, "De nullitate sententiae," *Apollinaris*, II (1929), 76-78.

Serédi, "De valore iuridico fontium Codicis I.C.," *Jus Pontificium*, I (1921), 63-66.

Periodicals

Apollinaris, Romae, 1928-

Jus Pontificium, Romae, 1921-1940.

Periodica de Religiosis et Missionariis, Brugis 1905-1919; *Periodica de Re Canonica et Morali Utili praesertim Religiosis et Missionariis*, Brugis, 1920-1927; *Periodica de Re Morali, Canonica, Liturgica*, Brugis, 1927-1936; Romae, 1937-.

Commentarium pro Religiosis, Romae, 1920-1934; ab anno 1935; *Commentarium pro Religiosis et Missionariis*.

ABBREVIATIONS

AAS—*Acta Apostolicae Sedis.*
Bruns—*Canones Apostolorum et Conciliorum Saeculorum IV-VII.*
Bull. Rom.—*Bullarium Romanum.*
Bull. Rom. Cont.—*Bullarii Romani* Continuatio.
C.—Codex Iutinianus, vel Causa.
c.—canon seu caput (iuris antiqui).
D.—Digesta.
Decisiones—*S. Romanae Rotae Decisiones seu Sententiae.*
Fontes—*Codicis Iuris Canonici Fontes.*
Jaffé—*Regesta Pontificium Romanorum ad annum MCXCVIII* (edited by Ewald, Kaltenbrunner, Löwenfeld).
Mansi—*Sacrorum Conciliorum Nova et Amplissima Collectio.*
MGH—*Monumenta Germaniae Historica.*
N.—Novellae.
Potthast—*Regesta Pontificium Romanorum ab anno MCXCVIII ad annum MCCCIV.*
S.C.C.—Sacra Congregatio Concilii.
S.C. de Sacramentis—Sacra Congregatio de disciplina Sacramentorum.
S.R.R.—Sacra Romana Rota.

BIOGRAPHICAL NOTE

John J. Noone was born on September 11, 1919, in Lost Creek, Pennsylvania. He attended St. Mary Magdalen's Parochial School there and Shenandoah Catholic High School. On September 1, 1938, he entered Saint Charles Seminary, Overbrook, Pennsylvania, where he received the Degree of Bachelor of Arts in 1943. He was ordained to the priesthood on May 30, 1946. The following October he entered the Catholic University of America to pursue graduate studies in the School of Canon Law. He received the Baccalaureate Degree in Canon Law in June, 1947, and the Degree of the Licentiate of Canon Law in June, 1948.

ALPHABETICAL INDEX

Altimarus, Blasius, 15
Apostates
  right to litigate of, 67
Apostolic Constitutions, 15
Apparitors, 41
Assessors, 37
Attorney
  power of, 70 ff.
Auditors, 37

Baptism
  essential for juridic capacity, 49
Benefice, 60
Bill of complaint, 80
Bishops
  competence with regard to cases of, 27
  contentious cases involving, 28

Cardinals
  competence with regard to cases of, 27
Causae Maiores, 27
Clarendon, parliament of, 6
Collegiate tribunal, 37
Competence, judicial
  definition of, 26
Contempt of Court, 31
Convalidation
  of an invalid process by Supreme Pontiff, 19
Councils
  II General Council of Lyons, 8
  of Vienne, 13
Couriers, 41
Criminal Cases
  requiring collegiate tribunal, 38

D'Angelo
  opinion of in regards to canons 1892 and 1894, 109
Decretals
  Legislation on nullity in, 5 ff.
  Pseudo-Isidorian, 2, 4
Defendant
  Obligation to respond, 51, 68
Defender of the Bond
  office of, 40
  presence required in matrimonial cases, 17, 105

Delegated jurisdiction, 21
DeLuca, 15
Diocese
  cases involving, 28
Durandus, 10, 12

English law
  and the right of patronage, 6
Error expressed in sentence, 11 ff.
Essential elements of a trial
  decretal law, 8
  pre-code jurisprudence regarding, 14
Exception
  of suspicion, 33
  validity of judicial acts pending settlement of, 34
Excommunicated
  right to litigate of, 66
Excommunication
  disqualification of in Decree of Gratian, 3
  in Decretal law, 7
  not invalidating procedure, 8, 9, 66
  jurisdiction of an excommunicated judge, 20

Fatalia legis, 42

Glossators, 10
Gonzalez-Tellez, 11
Governor
  forum for cases involving, 27
Gratian, 2
  essential judicial order, 3
Guardian
  right to appear in court 52 ff.

Heretics
  right to litigate, 67
Holy Office
  and the right of non-Catholics to introduce matrimonial cases, 50

Incompetence, 25
  absolute or relative, 26
  according to Gratian, 3
  decretal law, 5 ff.
  functional, 30
  obligation of judge to declare, 33

Roman law, 1
when the right of patronage is involved, 6
Infidels
disqualified for ecclesiastical jurisdiction, 19
lack juridic capacity, 49
Insane
procedural capacity of, 53
Interpretation of canons 1892 and 1894, 105
Ius standi in iudicio, 1, 49

Joinder of Issue, 93
Judge, 36
competence of in decretal law, 5
deficient jurisdiction of, 19 ff.
delegated, 7, 21 ff.
excommunicated, suspended, etc., 20
outside his own territory, 44
posture of, 10, 16
Juridic capacity, 49
Jurisdiction, judicial, 19 ff.
delegated, 21 ff.
territorial limits of, 43 ff.
Jurisprudence regarding nullity,
pre-code, 13
Rotal, 113

Legates
competence with regard to cases of, 27
Legitimation to act in a certain case, 49, 64
not always for validity, 69
Lieutenant-governor
forum for cases involving, 27
Litigants, 49

Mandate
of a delegated judge, 23
of a procurator, 8, 15, 70 ff.
Maranta, Robert, 15
Marriage
cases involving bond of, 38
right to attack validity of, 65, 69
Minors
procedural capacity of, 152
Monastic congregations
cases involving, 28
Moral persons
cases of, 128
juridic capacity of, 51
non-collegiate, 59
procedural capacity of, 58
religious, 63
secular, 61

Non-Catholic
may introduce summary cases, 50
plaintiff in matrimonial cases, 50, 68
right to litigate, 67
Notary, 21, 39, 105
Nullity
competence of judge to receive complaint of, 30
interpretation of canons on, 105 ff.
irremediable, 101
remediable, 101
sanation of, 105
tenor of present legislation regarding, 119

Officialis
and the delegation of his powers, 21, 22
appointment of, 36
Ordinary, local,
contentious cases involving, 28
judicial power of, 36
right to litigate in the name of moral persons under his jurisdiction, 59
right to represent cathedral church and episcopal mensal fund, 59
Ordination
cases involving bond of, 38

Papal States
limitation of grounds for nullity, in tribunals of, 14
Patronage, right of
controversy with English law concerning, 6
Pauline Privilege, 30
Place of the trial, 43, 86
pre-code law, 8
privilege of exempt places, 45
Popes
Alexander III, 11
Boniface VIII, 14
Clement V, 13
Gregory the Great, St., 2, 3
Gregory X, 8
Innocent III, 5, 13
Potiers
Judicial practice in the diocese of, 5
Prejudicial attempts against the rights of litigants, 32, 34, 42, 97, 99, 106
President
forum for cases involving, 27

Procurators
  mandate of, 8, 15, 70 ff.
  unauthorized, 70 ff.
Procedural capacity, 49, 51
Prodigals, 53
Promoter of Justice, 40, 66, 105
Proof introduced after the closing of the case, 100, 105

Ratification
  of the acts of an unauthorized representative, 64, 79
Record of the trial, 46
Religious, procedural capacity of, 56
Religious Communities
  cases involving, 28
  procedural capacity of, 63
Renouncement, judicial, 95, 105
Restitutio in integrum
  competent to grant, 31
  use of when procedural law violated, 106, 108
Roberti's interpretation of canons 1892 and 1894, 107
Roman Curia, as party litigant, 29
Roman law, 1
  legislation of incorporated into the Decree of Gratian, 5
  ius constitutionis et ius litigatoris, 10, 13
Roman Pontiff
  cases reserved to, 28
  competence of, 25, 30
  incompetence of others to judge, 26
Rota, Sacred Roman
  Jurisprudence of in regard to canons 1892 and 1894, 106, 113

Scabini, 6
Schismatics, right to litigate of, 67
Sentence
  contrary to law, 10 ff.
  execution of, 31
  extrinsic and intrinsic validity of, 16
  manifestly unjust, 10, 12
  nullity of, 101 ff.
  written, 16, 46
Signatures, 48, 104
Summary process, 13
  petition for by non-Catholic, 50
Summons, judicial, 81
  contents of, 83
  initial summons referred to in 1892, 103
  issued to plaintiff, 92
  service of, 88

Temporal rights and good
  of the bishop, 59
  of the cathedral church, 38, 59
Time of the trial, 42
  pre-code law, 8, 16
  terms of postponement, 42

Vantius, 14
Vicar-General, 21, 36
Vice-officiales, 22
Vice president, forum for cases involving, 27

Writing, 46, 106
  pre-code law, 9, 16
Weak-minded persons, 53
Women, disqualified for possessing ecclesiastical jurisdiction, 19

CANON LAW STUDIES*

1. Freriks, Rev. Celestine A., C.PP.S., J.C.D., Religious Congregations in Their External Relations, 121 pp., 1916.
2. Galliher, Rev. Daniel M., O.P., J.C.D., Canonical Elections, 117 pp., 1917.
3. Borkowski, Rev. Aurelius L., O.F.M., J.C.D., De Confraternitatibus Ecclesiasticis, 136 pp., 1918.
4. Castillo, Rev. Cayo, J.C.D., Disertacion Historico-Canonica sobre la Potestad del Cabildo en Sede Vacante o Impedida del Vicario Capitular, 99 pp., 1919 (1918).
5. Kubelbeck, Rev. William J., S.T.B., J.C.D., The Sacred Penitentiaria and Its Relation to Faculties of Ordinaries and Priests, 129 pp., 1918.
6. Petrovits, Rev. Joseph J. C., S.T.D., J.C.D., The New Church Law on Matrimony, X-461 pp., 1919.
7. Hickey, Rev. John J., S.T.B., J.C.D., Irregularities and Simple Impediments in the New Code of Canon Law, 100 pp., 1920.
8. Klekotka, Rev. Peter J., S.T.B., J.C.D., Diocesan Consultors, 179 pp., 1920.
9. Wanenmacher, Rev. Francis, J.C.D., The Evidence in Ecclesiastical Procedure Affecting the Marriage Bond, 1920 (Printed 1935).
10. Golden, Rev. Henry Francis, J.C.D., Parochial Benefices in the New Code, IV-119 pp., 1921 (Printed 1925).
11. Koudelka, Rev. Charles J., J.C.D., Pastors, Their Rights and Duties According to the New Code of Canon Law, 211 pp., 1921.
12. Melo, Rev. Antonius, O.F.M., J.C.D., De Exemptione Regularium, X-188 pp., 1921.
13. Schaaf, Rev. Valentine Theodore, O.F.M., S.T.B., J.C.D., The Cloister, X-180 pp., 1921.
14. Burke, Rev. Thomas Joseph, S.T.D., J.C.D., Competence in Ecclesiastical Tribunals, IV-117 pp., 1922.
15. Leech, Rev. George Leo, J.C.D., A Comparative Study of the Constitution "Apostolicae Sedis" and the "Codex Juris Canonici," 179 pp., 1922.
16. Motry, Rev. Hubert Louis, S.T.D., J.C.D., Diocesan Faculties According to the Code of Canon Law, II-167 pp., 1922.

---

*All published numbers are available from the Catholic University of America Press, 620 Michigan Ave., N.E., Washington 17, D. C., except the following: Nos. 1-114 inclusive, 116, 118, 120, 121, 122, 123, 136, 153, 162, 182 and 198. But the following numbers, now reissued, are obtainable from *The Jurist*, The Catholic University of America, Washington 17, D. C., namely: Nos. 5, 7, 11, 17, 18, 19, 26, 28, 30, 31, 34, 42, 44, 51, 52 and 61.

17. Murphy, Rev. George Lawrence, J.C.D., Delinquencies and Penalties in the Administration and the Reception of the Sacraments, IV-121 pp., 1923.
18. O'Reilly, Rev. John Anthony, S.T.B., J.C.D., Ecclesiastical Sepulture in the New Code of Canon Law, II-129 pp., 1923.
19. Michalicka, Rev. Wenceslas Cyril, O.S.B., J.C.D., Judicial Procedure in Dismissal of Clerical Exempt Religious, 107 pp., 1923.
20. Dargin, Rev. Edward Vincent, S.T.B., J.C.D., Reserved Cases According to the Code of Canon Law, IV-103 pp., 1924.
21. Godfrey, Rev. John A., S.T.B., J.C.D., The Right of Patronage According to the Code of Canon Law, 153 pp., 1924.
22. Hagedorn, Rev. Francis Edward, J.C.D., General Legislation on Indulgences, II-154 pp., 1924.
23. King, Rev. James Ignatius, J.C.D., The Administration of the Sacraments to Dying Non-Catholics, V-141 pp., 1924.
24. Winslow, Rev. Francis Joseph, M.M., J.C.D., Vicars and Prefects Apostolic, IV-149 pp., 1924.
25. Correa, Rev. Jose Servelion, S.T.L., J.C.D., La Potestad Legislativa de la Iglesia Catolica, IV-127 pp., 1925.
26. Dugan, Rev. Henry Francis, A.M., J.C.D., The Judiciary Department of the Diocesan Curia, 87 pp., 1925.
27. Keller, Rev. Charles Frederick, S.T.B., J.C.D., Mass Stipends, 167 pp., 1925.
238. Paschang, Rev. John Linus, J.C.D., The Sacramentals According to the Code of Canon Law, 129 pp., 1925.
29. Piontek, Rev. Cyrillus, O.F.M., S.T.B., J.C.D., De Indulto Exclaustrationis necnon Saecularizationis, XIII-289 pp., 1925.
30. Kearney, Rev. Richard Joseph, S.T.B., J.C.D., Sponsors at Baptism According to the Code of Canon Law, IV-127 pp. 1925.
31. Bartlett, Rev. Chester Joseph, A.M., LL.B., J.C.D., The Tenure of Parochial Property in the United States of America, V-108 pp., 1926.
32. Kilker, Rev. Adrian Jerome, J.C.D., Extreme Unction, V-425 pp., 1926.
33. McCormick, Rev. Robert Emmett, J.C.D., Confessors of Religious, VIII-266 pp., 1926.
34. Miller, Rev. Newton Thomas, J.C.D., Founded Masses According to the Code of Canon Law, VII-93 pp., 1926.
35. Roelker, Rev. Edward G., S.T.D., J.C.D., Principles of Privilege According to the Code of Canon Law, XI-166 pp., 1926.
36. Bakalarczyk, Rev. Richardus, M.I.C., J.U.D., De Novitiatu, VIII-208 pp., 1927.
37. Pizzuti, Rev. Lawrence, O.F.M., J.U.L., De Parochis Religiosis, 1927. (Not Printed.)
38. Bliley, Rev. Nicholas Martin, O.S.B., J.C.D., Altars According to the Code of Canon Law, XIX-132 pp., 1927.

39. BROWN, MR. BRENDAN FRANCIS, A.B., LL.M., J.U.D., The Canonical Juristic Personality with Special Reference to its Status in the United States of America, V-212 pp., 1927.
40. CAVANAUGH, REV. WILLIAM THOMAS, C.P., J.U.D., The Reservation of the Blessed Sacrament, VIII-101 pp., 1927.
41. DOHENY, REV. WILLIAM J., C.S.C., A.B., J.U.D., Church Property: Modes of Acquisition, X-118 pp., 1927.
42. FELDHAUS, REV. ALOYSIUS H., C.PP.S., J.C.D., Oratories, IX-141 pp., 1927.
43. KELLY, REV. JAMES PATRICK, A.B., J.C.D., The Jurisdiction of the Simple Confessor, X-208 pp., 1927.
44. NEUBERGER, REV. NICHOLAS J., J.C.D., Canon 6 or the Relation of the Codex Juris Canonici to the Preceding Legislation, V-95 pp., 1927.
45. O'KEEFE, REV. GERALD MICHAEL, J.C.D., Matrimonial Dispensations, Powers of Bishops, Priests, and Confessors, VIII-232 pp., 1927.
46. QUIGLEY, REV. JOSEPH, A.M., A.B., J.C.D., Condemned Societies, 139 pp., 1927.
47. ZAPLOTNIK, REV. JOHANNES LEO, J.C.D., De Vicariis Foraneis, X-142 pp., 1927.
48. DUSKIE, REV. JOHN ALOYSIUS, A.B., J.C.D., The Canonical Status of the Orientals in the United States, VIII-196 pp., 1928.
49. HYLAND, REV. FRANCIS EDWARD, J.C.D., Excommunication, Its Nature, Historical Development and Effects, VIII-181 pp., 1928.
50. REINMANN, REV. GERALD JOSEPH, O.M.C., J.C.D., The Third Order Secular of Saint Francis, 201 pp., 1928.
51. SCHENK, REV. FRANCIS J., J.C.D., The Matrimonial Impediments of Mixed Religion and Disparity of Cult, XVI-318 pp., 1929.
52. COADY, REV. JOHN JOSEPH, S.T.D., J.U.D., A.M., The Appointment of Pastors, VIII-150 pp., 1929.
53. KAY, REV. THOMAS HENRY, J.C.D., Competence in Matrimonial Procedure, VIII-164 pp., 1929.
54. TURNER, REV. SIDNEY JOSEPH, C.P., J.U.D., The Vow of Poverty, XLIX-217 pp., 1929.
55. KEARNEY, REV. RAYMOND A., A.B., S.T.D., J.C.D., The Principles of Delegation, VII-149 pp., 1929.
56. CONRAN, REV. EDWARD JAMES, A.B., J.C.D., The Interdict, V-163 pp., 1930.
57. O'NEILL, REV. WILLIAM H., J.C.D., Papal Rescripts of Favor, VII-218 pp., 1930.
58. BASTNAGEL, REV. CLEMENT VINCENT, J.U.D., The Appointment of Parochial Adjutants and Assistants, XV-257 pp., 1930.
59. FERRY, REV. WILLIAM A., A.B., J.C.D., Stole Fees, V-136 pp., 1930.
60. COSTELLO, REV. JOHN MICHAEL, A.B., J.C.D., Domicile and Quasi-Domicile, VII-201 pp., 1930.
61. KREMER, REV. MICHAEL NICHOLAS, A.B., S.T.B., J.C.D., Church Support in the United States, VI-136 pp., 1930.

62. ANGULO, REV. LUIS, C.M., J.C.D., Legislation de la Iglesia sobre la intencion en la application de la Santa Misa, VII-104 pp., 1931.
63. FREY, REV. WOLFGANG NORBERT, O.S.B., A.B., J.C.D., The Act of Religious Profession, VIII-174 pp., 1931.
64. ROBERTS, REV. JAMES BRENDAN, A.B., J.C.D., The Banns of Marriage, XIV-140 pp., 1931.
65. RYDER, REV. RAYMOND ALOYSIUS, A.B., J.C.D., Simony, IX-151 pp., 1931.
66. CAMPAGNA, REV. ANGELO, Ph.D., J.U.D., Il Vicario Generale del Vescovo, VII-205 pp., 1931.
67. COX, REV. JOSEPH GODFREY, A.B., J.C.D., The Administration of Seminaries, VI-124 pp., 1931.
68. GREGORY, REV. DONALD J., J.U.D., The Pauline Privilege, XV-165 pp., 1931.
69. DONOHUE, REV. JOHN F., J.C.D., The Impediment of Crime, VII-110 pp., 1931.
70. DOOLEY, REV. EUGENE A., O.M.I., J.C.D., Church Law on Sacred Relics, IX-143 pp., 1931.
71. ORTH, REV. CLEMENT RAYMOND, O.M.C., J.C.D., The Approbation of Religious Institutes, 171 pp., 1931.
72. PERNICONE, REV. JOSEPH M., A.B., J.C.D., The Ecclesiastical Prohibition of Books, XII-267 pp., 1932.
73. CLINTON, REV. CONNELL, A.B., J.C.D., The Paschal Precept, IX-108 pp., 1932.
74. DONNELLY, REV. FRANCIS B., A.M., S.T.L., J.C.D., The Diocesan Synod, VIII-125 pp., 1932.
75. TORRENTE, REV. CAMILO, C.M.F., J.C.D., Las Procesiones Sagradas, V-145 pp., 1932.
76. MURPHY, REV. EDWIN J., C.PP.S., J.C.D., Suspension Ex Informata Conscientia, XI-122 pp., 1932.
77. MACKENZIE, REV. ERIC F., A.M., S.T.L., J.C.D., The Delict of Heresy in its Commission, Penalization, Absolution, VII-124 pp., 1932.
78. LYONS, REV. AVITUS E., S.T.B., J.C.D., The Collegiate Tribunal of First Instance, XI-147 pp., 1932.
79. CONNOLLY, REV. THOMAS A., J.C.D., Appeals, XI-195 pp., 1932.
80. SANGMEISTER, REV. JOSEPH V., A.B., J.C.D., Force and Fear as Precluding Matrimonial Consent, V-211 pp., 1932.
81. JAEGER, REV. LEO A., A.B., J.C.D., The Administration of Vacant and Quasi-Vacant Episcopal Sees in the United States, IX-229 pp., 1932.
82. RIMLINGER, REV. HERBERT T., J.C.D., Error Invalidating Matrimonial Consent, VII-79 pp., 1932.
83. BARRETT, REV. JOHN D. M., S.S., J.C.D., A Comparative Study of the Plenary Councils of Baltimore and the Code of Canon Law, IX-221 pp., 1932.
84. CARBERRY, REV. JOHN J., Ph.D., S.T.D., J.C.D., The Juridical Form of Marriage, X-177 pp., 1934.

85. Dolan, Rev. John L., A.B., J.C.D., The Defensor Vinculi, XII-157 pp., 1934.
86. Hannan, Rev. Jerome D., A.M., S.T.D., LL.B., J.C.D., The Canon Law of Wills, IX-517 pp., 1934.
87. Lemieux, Rev. Delise A., A.M., J.C.D., The Sentence in Ecclesiastical Procedure, IX-131 pp., 1934.
88. O'Rourke, Rev. James J., A.B., J.C.D., Parish Registers, VII-109 pp., 1934.
89. Timlin, Rev. Bartholomew, O.F.M., A.M., J.C.D., Conditional Matrimonial Consent, X-381 pp., 1934.
90. Wahl, Rev. Francis X., A.B., J.C.D., The Matrimonial Impediments of Consanguinity and Affinity, VI-125 pp., 1934.
91. White, Rev. Robert J., A.B., LL.B., S.T.B., J.C.D., Canonical Ante-Nuptial Promises and the Civil Law, VI-152 pp., 1934.
92. Herrera, Rev. Antonio Parra, O.C.D., J.C.D., Legislacion Ecclesiastica sobra el Ayuno y la Abstinencia, XI-191 pp., 1935.
93. Kennedy, Rev. Edwin J., J.C.D., The Special Matrimonial Process in Cases of Evident Nullity, X-165 pp., 1935.
94. Manning, Rev. John J., A.B., J.C.D., Presumption of Law in Matrimonial Procedure, XI-111 pp., 1935.
95. Moeder, Rev. John M., J.C.D., The Proper Bishop for Ordination and Dimissorial Letters, VII-135 pp., 1935.
96. O'Mara, Rev. William A., A.B., J.C.D., Canonical Causes for Matrimonial Dispensations, IX-155 pp., 1935.
97. Reilly, Rev. Peter, J.C.D., Residence of Pastors, IX-81 pp., 1935.
98. Smith, Rev. Mariner T., O.P., S.T.Lr., J.C.D., The Penal Law for Religious, VII-169 pp., 1935.
99. Whalen, Rev. Donald W., A.M., J.C.D., The Value of Testimonial Evidence in Matrimonial Procedure, XIII-297 pp., 1935.
100. Cleary, Rev. Joseph F., J.C.D., Canonical Limitations on the Alienation of Church Property, VIII-141 pp., 1936.
101. Glynn, Rev. John C., J.C.D., The Promoter of Justice, XX-337 pp., 1936.
102. Brennan, Rev. James H., S.S., M.A., S.T.B., J.C.D., The Simple Convalidation of Marriage, VI-135 pp., 1937.
103. Brunini, Rev. Joseph Bernard, J.C.D., The Clerical Obligations of Canons 139 and 142, X-121 pp., 1937.
104. Connor, Rev. Maurice, A.B., J.C.D., The Administrative Removal of Pastors, VIII-159 pp., 1937.
105. Guilfoyle, Rev. Merlin Joseph, J.C.D., Custom, XI-144 pp., 1937.
106. Hughes, Rev. James Austin, A.B., A.M., J.C.D., Witnesses in Criminal Trials of Clerics, IX-140 pp., 1937.
107. Jansen, Rev. Raymond J., A.B., S.T.L., J.C.D., Canonical Provisions for Catechetical Instruction, VII-153 pp., 1937.
108. Kealy, Rev. John James, A.B., J.C.D., The Introductory Libellus in Church Court Procedure, XI-131 pp., 1937.

109. McManus, Rev. James Edward, C.Ss.R., J.C.D., The Administration of Temporal Goods in Religious Institutes, XVI-196 pp., 1937.
110. Moriarty, Rev. Eugene James, J.C.D., Oaths in Ecclesiastical Courts, X-115 pp., 1937.
111. Rainer, Rev. Eligius George, C.Ss.R., J.C.D., Suspension of Clerics, XVII-249 pp., 1937.
112. Reilly, Rev. Thomas F., C.Ss.R., J.C.D., Visitation of Religious, VI-195 pp., 1938.
113. Moriarity, Rev. Francis E., C.Ss.R., J.C.D., The Extraordinary Absolution from Censures, XV-334 pp., 1938.
114. Connolly, Rev. Nicholas P., J.C.D., The Canonical Erection of Parishes, X-132 pp., 1938.
115. Donovan, Rev. James Joseph, J.C.D., The Pastor's Obligation in Prenuptial Investigation, XII-322 pp., 1938.
116. Harrigan, Rev. Robert J., M.A., S.T.B., J.C.D., The Radical Sanation of Invalid Marriages, VIII-208 pp., 1938.
117. Boffa, Rev. Conrad Humbert, J.C.D., Canonical Provisions for Catholic Schools, VII-211 pp., 1939.
118. Parsons, Rev. Anscar John, O.M.Cap., J.C.D., Canonical Elections, XII-236 pp., 1939.
119. Reilly, Rev. Edward Michael, A.B., J.C.D., The General Norms of Dispensation, XII-156 pp., 1939.
120. Ryan, Rev. Gerald Aloysius, A.B., J.C.D., Principles of Episcopal Jurisdiction, XIII-172 pp., 1939.
121. Burton, Rev. Francis James, C.S.C., A.B., J.C.D., A Commentary on Canon 1125, X-222 pp., 1940.
122. Miaskiewicz, Rev. Francis Sigismund, J.C.D., Supplied Jurisdiction According to Canon 209, XII-340 pp., 1940.
123. Rice, Rev. Patrick William, A.B., J.C.D., Proof of Death in Prenuptial Investigation, VIII-156 pp., 1940.
124. Anglin, Rev. Thomas Francis, M.S., J.C.D., The Eucharistic Fast, VIII-183 pp., 1941.
125. Coleman, Rev. John Jerome, J.C.D., The Minister of Confirmation, VI-153 pp., 1941.
126. Downs, Rev. Joseph Emmanuel, A.B., J.C.D., The Concept of Clerical Immunity, XI-163 pp., 1941.
127. Esswein, Rev. Anthony Albert, J.C.D., Extrajudicial Penal Powers of Ecclesiastical Superiors, X-144 pp., 1941.
128. Farrell, Rev. Benjamin Francis, M.A., S.T.L., J.C.D., The Rights and Duties of the Local Ordinary Regarding Congregations of Women Religious of Pontifical Approval, V-195 pp., 1941.
129. Feeney, Rev. Thomas John, A.B., S.T.L., J.C.D., Restitutio in Integrum, VI-169 pp., 1941.
130. Findlay, Rev. Stephen William, O.S.B., A.B., J.C.D., Canonical Norms Governing the Deposition and Degradation of Clerics, XVII-279 pp., 1941.

131. Goodwine, Rev. John, A.B., S.T.L., J.C.D., The Right of the Church to Acquire Property, VIII-119 pp., 1941.
132. Heston, Rev. Edward Louis, C.S.C., Ph.D., S.T.D., J.C.D., The Alienation of Church Property in the United States, XII-222 pp., 1941.
133. Hogan, Rev. James John, A.B., S.T.L., J.C.D., Judicial Advocates and Procurators, XIII-200 pp., 1941.
134. Kealy, Rev. Thomas M., A.B., Litt.D., J.C.D., Dowry of Women Religious, IX-152 pp., 1941.
135. Keene, Rev. Michael James, O.S.B., J.C.D., Religious Ordinaries and Canon 198, V-164 pp., 1941 (Printed 1942).
136. Kerin, Rev. Charles A., S.S., M.A., S.T.B., J.C.D., The Privation of Christian Burial, XVI-279 pp., 1941.
137. Louis, Rev. William Francis, M.A., J.C.D., Diocesan Archives, X-101 pp., 1941.
138. McDevitt, Rev. Gilbert Joseph, A.B., J.C.D., Legitimacy and Legitimation, X-247 pp., 1941.
139. McDonough, Rev. Thomas Joseph, A.B., J.C.D., Apostolic Administrators, X-217 pp., 1941.
140. Meier, Rev. Carl Anthony, A.B., J.C.D., Penal Administrative Procedure Against Negligent Pastors, XI-240 pp., 1941.
141. Schmidt, Rev. John Rogg, A.B., J.C.D., The Principles of Authentic Interpretation in Canon 17 of the Code of Canon Law, XII-331 pp., 1941.
142. Slafkosky, Rev. Andrew Leonard, A.B., J.C.D., The Canonical Episcopal Visitation of the Diocese, X-197 pp., 1941.
143. Swoboda, Rev. Innocent Robert, O.F.M., J.C.D., Ignorance in Relation to the Imputability of Delicts, IX-271 pp., 1941.
144. Dube, Rev. Arthur Joseph, A.B., J.C.D., The General Principles for the Reckoning of Time in Canon Law, VIII-299 pp., 1941.
145. McBride, Rev. James T., A.B., J.C.D., Incardination and Excardination of Seculars, XX-585 pp., 1941.
146. Krol, Rev. John T., J.C.D., The Defendant in Ecclesiastical Trials, XII-207 pp., 1942.
147. Comyns, Rev. Joseph J., C.Ss.R., A.B., J.C.D., Papal and Episcopal Administration of Church Property, XIV-155 pp., 1942.
148. Barry, Rev. Garrett Francis, O.M.I., J.C.D., Violation of the Cloister, XII-260 pp., 1942.
149. Bolduc, Rev. Gatien, C.S.V., A.B., S.T.L., J.C.D., Les Etudes dans les Religions Clericales, VIII-155 pp., 1942.
150. Boyles, Rev. David John, M.A., J.C.D., The Juridic Effects of Moral Certitude on Pre-Nuptial Guarantees, XII-188 pp., 1942.
151. Canavan, Rev. Walter Joseph, M.A., Litt.D., J.C.D., The Profession of Faith, XII-143 pp., 1942.
152. Desrochers, Rev. Bruno, A.B., Ph.L., S.T.B., J.C.D., Le Premier Concile Plenier de Quebec et le Code de Droit Canonique, XIV-186 pp., 1942.

153. DILLON, REV. ROBERT EDWARD, A.B., J.C.D., Common Law Marriage, X-148 pp., 1942.
154. DODWELL, REV. EDWARD JOHN, PH.D., S.T.B., J.C.D., The Time and Place for the Celebration of Marriage, X-156 pp., 1942.
155. DONNELLAN, REV. THOMAS ANDREW, A.B., J.C.D., The Obligation of the Missa pro Populo, VII-131 pp., 1942.
156. ELTZ, REV. LOUIS ANTHONY, A.B., J.C.D., Cooperation in Crime, XII-208 pp., 1942.
157. GASS, REV. SYLVESTER FRANCIS, M.A., J.C.D., Ecclesiastical Pensions, XI-206 pp., 1942.
158. GUINIVEN, REV. JOHN JOSEPH, C.Ss.R., J.C.D., The Precept of Hearing Mass, XIV-188 pp., 1942.
159. GULCZYNSKI, REV. JOHN THEOPHILUS, J.C.D., The Desecration and Violation of Churches, X-126 pp., 1942.
160. HAMMILL, REV. JOHN LEO, M.A., J.C.D., The Obligations of the Traveler According to Canon 14, VIII-204 pp., 1942.
161. HAYDT, REV. JOHN JOSEPH, A.B., J.C.D., Reserved Benefices, XI-148 pp., 1942.
162. HUSER, REV. ROGER JOHN, O.F.M., A.B., J.C.D., The Crime of Abortion in Canon Law, XII-187 pp., 1942.
163. KEARNEY, REV. FRANCIS PATRICK, A.B., S.T.L., J.C.D., The Principles of Canon 1127, X-162 pp., 1942.
164. LINAHEN, REV. LEO JAMES, S.T.L., J.C.D., De Absolutione Complicis in Peccato Turpi, 114 pp., 1942.
165. McCLOSKEY, REV. JOSEPH ALOYSIUS, A.B., J.C.D., The Subject of Ecclesiastical Law According to Canon 12, XVII-246 pp., 1942 (Printed 1943).
166. O'NEILL, REV. FRANCIS JOSEPH, C.Ss.R., J.C.D., The Dismissal of Religious in Temporary Vows, XIII-220 pp., 1942.
167. PRINCE, REV. JOHN EDWARD, A.B., S.T.D., J.C.D., The Diocesan Chancellor, X-136 pp., 1942.
168. RIESNER, REV. ALBERT JOSEPH, C.Ss.R., J.C.D., Apostates and Fugitives from Religious Institutes, IX-168 pp., 1942.
169. STENGER, REV. JOSEPH BERNARD, J.C.D., The Mortgaging of Church Property, 186 pp., 1942.
170. WALDRON, REV. JOSEPH FRANCIS, A.B., J.C.D., The Minister of Baptism, XII-197 pp., 1942.
171. WILLETT, REV. ROBERT ALBERT, J.C.D., The Probative Value of Documents in Ecclesiastical Trials, X-124 pp., 1942.
172. WOEBER, REV. EDWARD MARTIN, M.A., J.C.D., The Interpellations, XII-161 pp., 1942.
173. BENKO, REV. MATTHEW ALOYSIUS, O.S.B., M.A., J.C.D., The Abbot Nullius, XIV-148 pp., 1943.
174. CHRIST, REV. JOSEPH JAMES, M.A., S.T.L., J.C.D., Dispensation from Vindicative Penalties, XIV-285 pp., 1943.

175. CLANCY, REV. PATRICK M. J., O.P., A.B., S.T.Lr., J.C.D., The Local Religious Superior, X-299 pp., 1943.
176. CLARKE, REV. THOMAS JAMES, J.C.D., Parish Societies, XII-147 pp., 1943.
177. CONNOLLY, REV. JOHN PATRICK, S.T.L., J.C.D., Synodal Examiners and Parish Priest Consultors, X-223 pp., 1943.
178. DRUMM, REV. WILLIAM MARTIN, A.B., J.C.D., Hospital Chaplains, XII-175 pp., 1943.
179. FLANAGAN, REV. BERNARD JOSEPH, A.B., S.T.L., J.C.D., The Canonical Erection of Religious Houses, X-147 pp., 1943.
180. KELLEHER, REV. STEPHEN JOSEPH, A.B., S.T.B., J.C.D., Discussions with non-Catholics; Canonical Legislation, X-93 pp., 1943.
181. LEWIS, REV. GORDIAN, C.P., J.C.D., Chapters in Religious Institutes, XII-169 pp., 1943.
182. MARX, REV. ADOLPH, J.C.D., The Declaration of Nullity of Marriages Contracted Outside the Church, X-151 pp., 1943.
183. MATULENAS, REV. RAYMOND ANTHONY, O.S.B., A.B., J.C.D., Communication a Source of Privileges, XII-225 pp., 1943.
184. O'LEARY, REV. CHARLES GERARD, C.Ss.R., J.C.D., Religious Dismissed After Perpetual Profession, X-213 pp., 1943.
185. POWER, REV. CORNELIUS MICHAEL, J.C.D., The Blessing of Cemeteries. XII-231 pp., 1943.
186. SHUHLER, REV. RALPH VINCENT, O.S.A., J.C.D., Privileges of Regulars to Absolve and Dispense, XII-195 pp., 1943.
187. ZIOLKOWSKI, REV. THADDEUS STANISLAUS, A.B., J.C.D., The Consecration and Blessing of Churches, XII-151 pp., 1943.
188. HENEGHAN, REV. JOHN JOSEPH, S.T.D., J.C.D., The Marriages of Unworthy Catholics: Canons 1065 and 1066, XVI-213 pp., 1944.
189. CARROLL, REV. COLEMAN FRANCIS, M.C., S.T.L., J.C.L., Charitable Institutions.
190. CIESLUK, REV. JOSEPH EDWARD, Ph.B., S.T.L., J.C.D., National Parishes in the United States, VI-178 pp., 1944.
191. COBURN, REV. VINCENT PAUL, A.B., J.C.D., Marriages of Conscience, XII-172 pp., 1944.
192. CONNORS, REV. CHARLES PAUL, C.S.Sp., A.B., J.C.D., Extra-Judicial Procurators in the Code of Canon Law, X-94 pp., 1944.
193. COYLE, REV. PAUL RAYMOND, A.B., J.C.D., Judicial Exceptions, X-142 pp., 1944.
194. FAIR, REV. BARTHOLOMEW FRANCIS, A.B., S.T.L., J.C.D., The Impediment of Abduction, XII-122 pp., 1944.
195. GALLAGHER, REV. THOMAS RAPHAEL, O.P., A.B., S.T.Lr., J.C.D., The Examination of the Qualities of the Ordinand, X-166 pp., 1944.
196. GANNON, REV. JOHN MARK, S.T.L., J.C.D., The Interstices Required for the Promotion to Orders, XII-100 pp., 1944.

197. Goldsmith, Rev. J. William, B.C.S., S.T.L., J.C.D., The Competence of Church and State over Marriage—Disputed Points, X-128 pp., 1944.
198. Goodwine, Rev. Joseph Gerard, A.B., S.T.B., J.C.D., The Reception of Converts, XIV-326 pp., 1944.
199. Kowalski, Rev. Romuald Eugene, O.F.M., A.B., J.C.D., Sustenance of Religious Houses of Regulars, X-174 pp., 1944.
200. McCoy, Rev. Alan Edward, O.F.M., J.C.D., Force and Fear in Relation to Delictual Imputability and Penal Responsibility, XII-160 pp., 1944.
201. McDevitt, Rev. Vincent John, Ph.B., S.T.L., J.C.L., Perjury.
202. Martin, Rev. Thomas Owen, Ph.D., S.T.D., J.C.D., Adverse possession, Prescription and Limitation of Actions; The Canonical "Praescriptio," XX-208 pp., 1944.
203. Miklosovic, Rev Paul John, A.B., J.C.L., Attempted Marriages and Their Consequent Juridic Effects.
204. Mundy, Rev. Thomas Maurice, A.B., S.T.L., J.C.D., The Union of Parishes, X-164 pp., 1944.
205. O'Dea, Rev. John Coyle, A.B., J.C.D., The Matrimonial Impediment of Nonage, VIII-126 pp., 1944.
206. Olalia, Rev. Alexander Ayson, S.T.L., J.C.D., A Comparative Study of the Christian Constitution of States and the Constitution of the Philippine Commonwealth, XII-136 pp., 1944.
207. Poisson, Rev. Pierre-Marie, C.S.C., A.B., Ph.L., Th.L., J.C.L., Droits Patrimoniaux des Maisons et des Eglises Religieuses.
208. Stadalnikas, Rev. Casimir Joseph, M.I.C., J.C.D., Reservation of Censures, X-141 pp., 1944.
209. Sullivan, Rev. Eugene Henry, S.T.L., J.C.D., Proof of the Reception of the Sacraments, X-165 pp., 1944.
210. Vaughan, Rev. William Edward, J.C.D., Constitutions for Diocesan Courts, X-210 pp., 1944.
211. Paro, Rev. Gino, S.T.D., J.C.D., The Right of Papal Legation, X-221 pp., 1944 (Printed 1947).
212. Balzer, Rev. Ralph Francis, C.P., J.C.D., The Computation of Time in a Canonical Novitiate, X-227 pp., 1945.
213. Dougherty, Rev. John Whelan, A.B., S.T.L., J.C.D., De Inquisitione Speciali, XII-195 pp., 1945.
214. Dziob, Rev. Michael Walter, J.C.D., The Sacred Congregation for the Oriental Church, XII-181 pp., 1945.
215. Eidenschink, Rev. John Albert, O.S.B., B.A., J.C.D., The Election of Bishops in the Letters of Pope Gregory the Great, VIII-200 pp., 1945.
216. Gill, Rev. Nicholas, C.P., J.C.D., The Spiritual Prefect in Clerical Religious Houses of Study, X-140 pp., 1945.
217. Hynes, Rev. Harry Gerard, S.T.L., J.C.D., The Privileges of Cardinals, XII-183 pp., 1945.

218. McDevitt, Rev. Gerald Vincent, S.T.L., J.C.D., The Renunciation of an Ecclesiastical Office, XIV-179 pp., 1946.
219. Manning, Rev. Joseph Leroy, J.C.D., The Free Conferral of Offices. VII-116 pp., 1945.
220. Meyer, Rev. Louis G., O.S.B., A.B., S.T.B., J.C.D., Alms-Gathering by Religious, XII-163 pp., 1946.
221. O'Donnell, Rev. Cletus Francis, M.A., J.C.D., The Marriage of Minors, XII-268 pp., 1945.
222. Prunskis, Rev. Joseph, J.C.D., Comparative Law, Ecclesiastical and Civil in Lithuanian Concordat, X-161 pp., 1945.
223. Sweeney, Rev. Francis Patrick, C.Ss.R., J.C.D., The Reduction of Clerics to the Lay State, X-199 pp., 1945.
224. Vogelpohl, Rev. Henry John, J.C.D., The Simple Impediments to Holy Orders, XVI-190 pp., 1945.
225. Brockhaus, Rev. Thomas Aquinas, O.S.B., A.B., J.C.D., Religious who Are Known as Conversi, X-127 pp., 1945.
226. Griese, Rev. Nicholas Orville, S.T.D., J.C.D., Marriage and The Procreation of Offspring, XVI-224 pp., 1945.
227. Boudreaux, Rev. Warren Louis, J.C.D., The "ab acatholicis nati" of Canon 1099, § 2, XII-110 pp., 1946.
228. Bowe, Rev. Thomas Joseph, A.B., J.C.D., Religious Superioresses, VIII-206 pp., 1946.
229. Diederichs, Rev. Michael Ferdinand, S.C.J., J.C.D., The Jurisdiction of the Latin Ordinaries over their Oriental Subjects, XIV-153 pp., 1946.
230. Dingman, Rev. Maurice John, A.B., S.T.L., J.C.L., The Plaintiff in Contentious Trials.
231. Frison, Rev. Basil, C.M.F., M.Mus., J.C.D., The Retroactivity of Law, X-221 pp., 1946.
232. Galvin, Rev. William Anthony, M.A., J.C.D., The Administrative Transfer of Pastors, XII-288 pp., 1946.
233. Goracy, Rev. Joseph C., J.C.L., The Diriment Impediment of Major Orders.
234. Hale, Rev. Joseph Francis, M.A., S.T.L., J.C.D., The Pastor of Burial, X-247 pp., 1946 (Printed 1949).
235. Henry, Rev. Joseph Arthur, A.B., J.C.D., The Mass and Holy Communion: Inter-Ritual Law, XII-138 pp., 1946.
236. Linenberger, Rev. Herbert, C.PP.S., J.C.D., The False Denunciation of an Innocent Confession, VIII-205 pp., 1946 (Printed 1949).
237. Lowry, Rev. James Martin, A.B., J.C.D., Dispensation from Private Vows, XII-266 pp., 1946.
238. Lynch, Rev. George Edward, A.B., S.T.L., J.C.D., Coadjutors and Auxiliaries of Bishops, X-107 pp., 1946 (Printed 1947).
239. Lynch, Rev. Timothy, M.S.SS.T., J.C.D., Contracts between Bishops and Religious Congregations, XIV-232 pp., 1946.

240. McClunn, Rev. Justin David, A.B., S.T.L., J.C.D., Administrative Recourse, VII-142 pp., 1946.
241. Lohmuller, Rev. Martin M., A.B., J.C.D., The Promulgation of Law, XII-140 pp., 1947.
242. McGrath, Rev. James, A.B., J.C.D., The Privilege of the Canon, XII-156 pp., 1946.
243. Marbach, Rev. Joseph Francis, A.B., J.C.D., Marriage Legislation for the Catholics of the Oriental Rites in the United States and Canada, XIV-314 pp., 1946.
244. Shimkus, Rev. Bernard Aloysius, A.B., J.C.L., The Determination and Transfer of Rite.
245. Smith, Rev. Vincent Michael, A.B., S.T.L., J.C.L., Ignorance Affecting Matrimonial Consent.
246. Wachtrle, Rev. Paul Anthony, A.B., J.C.L., The Baptism of the Children of Non-Catholics.
247. Crotty, Rev. Matthew M., J.C.D., The Recipient of First Holy Communion, X-142 pp., 1947.
248. Eagleton, Rev. George, J.C.D., The Quinquennial Faculties, Formula IV, XIV-199 pp., 1947 (Printed 1948).
249. Gibbons, Rev. Marion L., C.M., LL.B., J.C.D., Domicile of The Wife Unlawfully Separated from Her Husband, XIV-171 pp., 1947.
250. Kelly, Rev. Bernard M., S.T.L., J.C.D., The Functions Reserved to Pastors, XII-141 pp., 1947.
251. Kilcullen, Rev. Thomas J., LL.M., J.C.D., The Collegiate Moral Person as Party Litigant, X-150 pp., 1947.
252. Lafontaine, Rev. Germain J., W.F., J.C.D., Relations Canoniques entre Le Missionnaire et Ses Superieurs, X-117 pp., 1947.
253. Lane, Rev. Loras T., A.B., S.T.L., J.C.L., Matrimonial Procedure in the Ordinary Court of Second Instance.
254. Lover, Rev. James F., C.Ss.R., J.C.D., The Master of Novices, X-168 pp., 1947.
255. McNicholas, Rev. Timothy J., J.C.L., The Septimae Manus Witness.
256. Marositz, Rev. Joseph J., M.S.C., J.C.D., Obligations and Privileges of Religious Promoted to the Episcopal or Cardinalitial Dignities, XII-180 pp., 1947.
257. Murphy, Rev. Francis J., A.B., J.C.D., Legislative Powers of the Provincial Council, XII-158 pp., 1947.
258. O'Brien, Rev. Romaeus W., O.Carm., J.C.D., The Provincial Superior in Religious Orders of Men, X-294 pp., 1947.
259. Pfaller, Rev. Benedict A., O.S.B., J.C.L., The Ipso Facto Effected Dismissal of Religious.
260. Popek, Rev. Alphonse S., M.A., J.C.D., The Rights and Obligations of Metropolitans, XVIII-460 pp., 1947.
261. Ristuccia, Rev. Bernard J., C.M., J.C.D., Quasi-Religious, XVI-318 pp., 1947 (Printed 1949).

262. SONNTAG, REV. NATHANIEL L., O.F.M.CAP., J.C.D., Censorship of Special Classes of Books, XII-147 pp., 1947.
263. STADLER, REV. JOSEPH N., J.C.L., Frequent Holy Communion.
264. SZAL, REV. IGNATIUS J., J.C.L., The Communication of Catholics with Schismatics.
265. WAGNER, REV. URBAN S., O.F.M. CONV., J.C.D., Parochial Substitute Vicars and Supplying Priests, IX-126 pp., 1947.
266. QUINN, REV. JOSEPH, M.A., J.C.L., Documents Required for the Reception of Orders.
267. BENNINGTON, REV. JAMES CLEMENT, A.B., J.C.L., The Recipient of Confirmation.
268. BLAHER, REV. DAMIAN JOSEPH, O.F.M., A.B., J.C.L., The Ordinary Processes in Causes of Beatification and Canonization.
269. CLUNE, REV. ROBERT BELL, A.B., J.C.L., The Judicial Interrogation of the Parties.
270. COURTMANCHE, REV. BASIL F., A.B., J.C.L., The Total Simulation of Matrimonial Consent.
271. DLOUHY, REV. MAUR JOHN, O.S.B., A.B., J.C.L., The Ordination of Exempt Religious.
272. DONOVAN, REV. JOHN THOMAS, PH.B., S.T.L., J.C.D., The Clerical Obligations of Canons 138 and 140, XII-209 pp., 1948.
273. FREKING REV. FREDERICK W., A.B., S.T.B., J.C.L., The Canonical Installation of Pastors.
274. FULTON, REV. THOMAS B., J.C.L., Prenuptial Investigation.
275. GODLEY, REV. JAMES P., J.C.L., The Time and the Place for the Celebration of Mass.
276. KANE, REV. THOMAS A., A.B., B.S., J.C.D., The Jurisdiction of the Patriarchs of the Major Sees in Antiquity and in the Middle Ages, XII-111 pp., 1948 (Printed 1949).
277. KENNEDY, REV. ANDREW A., J.C.L., The Annual Pastoral Report to the Local Ordinary.
278. KONRAD, REV. JOSEPH GEORGE, J.C.L., Transfer of Religious.
279. KRESS, REV. ALPHONSE, J.C.L., Contumacy in Ecclesiastical Trials.
280. MCCARTNEY, REV. MARCELLUS ANTHONY, O.F.M., M.A., J.C.L., Faculties of Regular Confessors.
281. MCCASLIN, REV. EDWARD PATRICK, M.A., S.T.L., J.C.L., The Division of Parishes.
282. MCELROY, REV. FRANCIS J., A.B., J.C.L., The Privileges of Bishops.
283. QUINN, REV. STEPHEN, M.S.SS.T., J.C.D., Relation between the Local Ordinary and Religious of Diocesan Approval, XII-158 pp., 1948 (Printed 1949).
284. SCHNEIDER, REV. EDELHARD LOUIS, A.D.S., M.A., J.C.D., The Status of Secularized ex-Religious Clerics, X-155 pp., 1948.
285. THOMPSON, REV. CHESTER J., A.B., J.C.L., The Simple Removal from Office.

286. O'Brien, Rev. Kenneth R., A.B., J.C.D., The Nature of Support of Diocesan Priests in the United States, XVI-162 pp., 1949.
287. Metz, Rev. John E., S.T.L., J.C.D., The Recording Judge in the Ecclesiastical Collegiate Tribunal, X-130 pp., 1949.
288. Reinhardt, Rev. Marion J., S.T.L., J.C.L., The Rogatory Commission.
289. Ortega Uhink, Rev. Juan, S.J., J.C.L., *De Delicto Sollicitationis.*
290. Casey, Rev. James V., J.C.L., A Study of Canon 2222, § 1.
291. Allgeier, Rev. Joseph L., J.C.L., The Canonical Obligations of Preaching in Parish Churches.
292. Cahill, Rev. Daniel R., J.C.L., The Custody of the Holy Eucharist.
293. Carr, Rev. Aidan, O.F.M., Conv., S.T.D., J.C.L., Vocation to the Priesthood: Its Canonical Concept.
294. Knopke, Rev. Roch F., O.F.M., J.C.L., Reverential Fear in Matrimonial Cases in Asiatic Countries: Rota Cases.
295. Lavelle, Rev. Howard D., J.C.L., The Obligation of Holding Sacred Missions in Parishes.
296. Michells, Rev. Anthony B., J.C.L., The Constitutive Elements of Parishes.
297. Noone, Rev. John J., J.C.L., Nullity in Judicial Acts.
298. Sheehan, Rev. Daniel E., J.C.L., The Minister of Holy Communion.
299. Statkus, Rev. Francis J., J.C.L., The Minister of the Last Sacraments.
300. Cook, Rev. John P., J.C.L., Ecclesiastical Communities and Their Ability to Induce Legal Customs.
301. Fazzalaro, Rev. Francis J., J.C.L., The Place for the Hearing of Confessions.
302. Hannan, Rev. Philip M., J.C.L., The Canonical Concept of *Congrua Sustentatio* for the Secular Clergy.
303. Quinn, Rev. Hugh G., S.T.L., J.C.L., The Particular Penal Precept.
304. Gallagher, Rev. John F., J.C.L., The Matrimonial Impediment of Public Propriety.
305. Welsh, Rev. Thomas J., J.C.L., The Use of the Portable Altar.

www.ingramcontent.com/pod-product-compliance
Lightning Source LLC
LaVergne TN
LVHW050218080826
844660LV00012B/434

* 9 7 8 0 8 1 3 2 2 4 7 3 2 *